THE NEW
COOK

THE NEW
COOK

MARY BERRY

PHOTOGRAPHY DAVE KING

DORLING KINDERSLEY
LONDON • NEW YORK • SYDNEY • MOSCOW

A Dorling Kindersley Book

Editorial & Cookery Consultant Jeni Wright
Editor Nicky Vimpany
Assistant Editor Lorraine Turner
Art Editors Colin Robson, Rosamund Saunders
Design Assistant Clare Marshall
DTP Designer Bridget Roseberry
Managing Editor Mary Ling
Deputy Art Director Carole Ash
Production Controller Martin Croshaw

First published in Great Britain in 1997 by
Dorling Kindersley Limited,
9 Henrietta Street, London WC2E 8PS
2 4 6 8 10 9 7 5 3

CONTENTS

STORECUPBOARD 10

*Advice on how to create a stock of useful ingredients
that you can call on from day to day.*

EQUIPMENT 20

*A practical guide to avoiding expensive mistakes
when equipping your kitchen.*

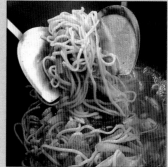

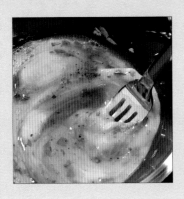
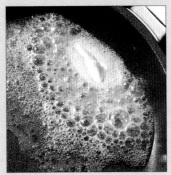
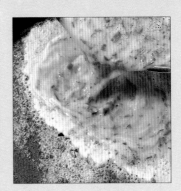
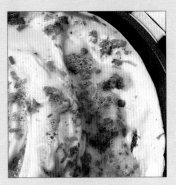

TECHNIQUES 32

These techniques are the building blocks the beginner will use to construct the recipes that follow. Mastering these simple basic skills will ensure culinary success now and for many years to come.

MASTER RECIPES 72

Each of these Master Recipes is fully explained in step-by-step pictures, with information on special equipment and ingredients, and cook's tips from the expert.

RECIPE REPERTOIRE 118

A resource of essential recipes for the new cook, drawing on the skills learnt in the Techniques and Master Recipes sections to create an impressive culinary range.

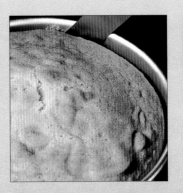

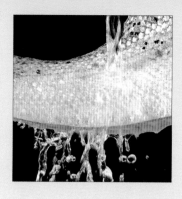

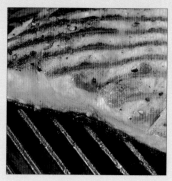

INTRODUCTION

THIS IS THE FIRST BOOK I've written for the new cook, and I had a great incentive – it is especially for Sarah, our brand new daughter-in-law, who is very keen to cook. She has been with me, looking over my shoulder while I have been developing and testing the recipes – and our son Tom can't wait for the results.

I have a real soft spot for people who are just beginning to cook, and I want them to have fun with cooking and enjoy the results. For the novice, even opening a recipe book can be incredibly daunting, so my aim with this book is to make cooking as easy and uncomplicated as possible.

I must say how much I've enjoyed going right back to the beginning, thinking about the basics and approaching them with a fresh eye for today's new cooks who want fresher, lighter food.

I start with a visual guide to the kitchen storecupboard, describing and explaining a key choice of ingredients from peppercorns, oils and vinegars, to pasta and pulses, vanilla pods and honey. A store of good, basic ingredients will help you cook well, and for those on a budget, this section will ensure that bad buys are kept to a minimum, and correct storage prevents unnecessary waste.

Many new cooks have little money to spare for setting up a kitchen. To help you avoid expensive mistakes, I have devoted a section to kitchen tools and equipment. It will allow you to identify which items are most practical and versatile, and which items are worth investing in for the long term. Why

buy a cheap set of bad knives when just two or three good ones will do, and will last for ever? Which is the most useful electrical equipment to buy? Good-quality machines are expensive, so you need to choose wisely.

A portfolio of essential Techniques forms a vital reference source. From cracking eggs and peeling potatoes, to determining roasting times for poultry and meat, this is the basic know-how section you will turn to again and again over the years.

The twelve Master Recipes are designed to get you off to a good start. These will be your master keys, opening up a collection of basic, but essential, cooking skills. How to make a fluffy omelette and a creamy soup, how to pan-fry chops and grill vegetables, roast a chicken, make an apple pie and a teatime cake – and more. All are easy to follow, with precise instructions and beautiful step-by-step photographs. With these recipes, you will be able to cook with confidence, for everyday and special occasions.

Last but not least, there is the Recipe Repertoire, a collection of my favourite recipes that I hope will become yours too. Here you will find some time-honoured classics with a modern twist, and some new and imaginative ideas using the latest ingredients available in our supermarkets.

A very special thank you goes to Caroline Liddell, who prepared the food so beautifully for the photographs and was an inspiration with her recipe testing, and to my editor Jeni Wright, who has kept me laughing as we both juggle our family lives with demanding careers.

Mary Berry

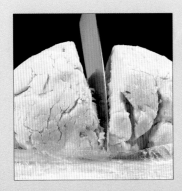

HOW TO USE THIS BOOK

The sections of this book are designed to be used in conjunction

with each other: always read all the relevant information through

before you begin. All recipes serve four unless otherwise stated.

■ MASTER RECIPES

These twelve Master Recipes use the basic techniques
shown in the Techniques section and teach the new cook
the key skills they will need to build up a whole culinary
repertoire. We recommend that you start with these recipes.

*Each Master Recipe has a close up
shot to inspire you and to show you
exactly what you should expect to see
as your dish progresses.*

*The Keys to Success
contain vital information.
Read them carefully
before you begin.*

*Cook's Notes contains tips
on preparation, serving
and nutritional values.*

*Cross-references to all the
techniques you will need
appear in the bottom left-
hand corner of the page.*

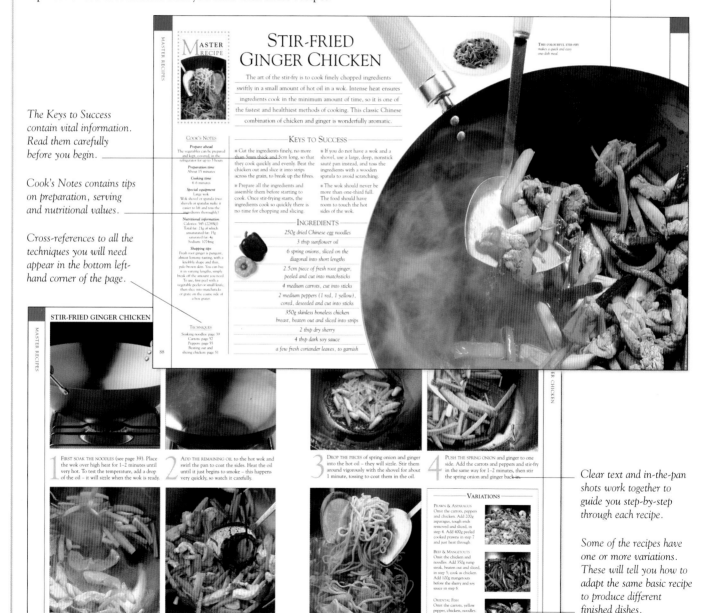

MASTER RECIPE

STIR-FRIED GINGER CHICKEN

The art of the stir-fry is to cook finely chopped ingredients
swiftly in a small amount of hot oil in a wok. Intense heat ensures
ingredients cook in the minimum amount of time, so it is one of
the fastest and healthiest methods of cooking. This classic Chinese
combination of chicken and ginger is wonderfully aromatic.

*THIS COLOURFUL STIR-FRY
makes a quick and easy
one-dish meal.*

COOK'S NOTES

Prepare ahead
The vegetables can be prepared
and kept, covered, in the
refrigerator for up to 3 hours.

Preparation time
About 15 minutes

Cooking time
4–6 minutes

Special equipment
Large wok
Wok shovel or spatula (two
shovels or spatulas make it
easier to lift and toss the
ingredients thoroughly)

Nutritional information
Calories: 545 (2289kJ)
Total fat: 21g of which
unsaturated fat: 15g
saturated fat: 4g
Sodium: 1074mg

Shopping tips
Fresh root ginger is pungent,
almost lemony-tasting, with a
knobbly shape and thin,
pale-brown skin. You can buy
it in varying lengths, simply
break off the amount you need.
To use, first peel with a
vegetable peeler or small knife,
then slice into matchsticks
or grate on the coarse side of
a box grater.

KEYS TO SUCCESS

■ Cut the ingredients finely, no more
than 5mm thick and 5cm long, so that
they cook quickly and evenly. Beat the
chicken out and slice it into strips
across the grain, to break up the fibres.

■ Prepare all the ingredients and
assemble them before starting to
cook. Once stir-frying starts, the
ingredients cook so quickly there is
no time for chopping and slicing.

■ If you do not have a wok and a
shovel, use a large, deep, nonstick
sauté pan instead, and toss the
ingredients with a wooden
spatula to avoid scratching.

■ The wok should never be
more than one-third full.
The food should have
room to touch the hot
sides of the wok.

INGREDIENTS

250g dried Chinese egg noodles

3 tbsp sunflower oil

6 spring onions, sliced on the
diagonal into short lengths

2.5cm piece of fresh root ginger,
peeled and cut into matchsticks

4 medium carrots, cut into matchsticks

2 medium peppers (1 red, 1 yellow),
cored, deseeded and cut into sticks

350g skinless boneless chicken
breast, beaten out and sliced into strips

2 tbsp dry sherry

4 tbsp dark soy sauce

a few fresh coriander leaves, to garnish

TECHNIQUES
Soaking noodles: page 39
Carrots: page 57
Peppers: page 55
Beating out and
slicing chicken: page 51

88

STIR-FRIED GINGER CHICKEN

1 FIRST SOAK THE NOODLES (see page 39). Place
the wok over high heat for 1–2 minutes until
very hot. To test the temperature, add a drop
of the oil – it will sizzle when the wok is ready.

2 ADD THE REMAINING OIL to the hot wok and
swirl the pan to coat the sides. Heat the oil
until it just begins to smoke – this happens
very quickly, so watch it carefully.

3 DROP THE PIECES of spring onion and ginger
into the hot oil – they will sizzle. Stir them
around vigorously with the shovel for about
1 minute, tossing to coat them in the oil.

4 PUSH THE SPRING ONION and ginger to one
side. Add the carrots and peppers and stir-fry
in the same way for 1–2 minutes, then stir
the spring onion and ginger back in.

*Clear text and in-the-pan
shots work together to
guide you step-by-step
through each recipe.*

*Some of the recipes have
one or more variations.
These will tell you how to
adapt the same basic recipe
to produce different
finished dishes.*

5 PUSH THE VEGETABLES aside and add the
chicken a little at a time. Sizzle the chicken
briefly on each side before tossing with the
other ingredients for a further 1–2 minutes.

6 POUR IN THE SHERRY and allow it to bubble
briefly (this burns off the alcohol but
maintains flavour). Add the soy sauce and
stir to mix with the chicken and vegetables.

7 DRAIN THE NOODLES (see page 39), add to
the wok and toss to mix. Taste and add more
soy sauce if you like. Serve immediately,
sprinkled with coriander leaves.

VARIATIONS

PRAWN & ASPARAGUS
Omit the carrots, peppers
and chicken. Add 200g
asparagus, tough ends
removed and sliced, in
step 4. Add 400g peeled
cooked prawns in step 7
and just heat through.

BEEF & MANGETOUTS
Omit the chicken and
noodles. Add 350g rump
steak, beaten out and sliced,
in step 5; cook as chicken.
Add 100g mangetouts
before the sherry and soy
sauce in step 6.

ORIENTAL FISH
Omit the carrots, yellow
pepper, chicken, noodles.
Use 2 red peppers, sliced,
in step 4. Add 350g
skinned cod fillet, cut into
chunks, with 250g Chinese
lettuce, shredded, in step 5.

90

91

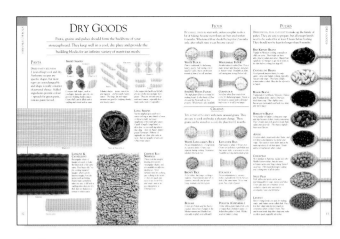

■ EQUIPMENT

All the recipes in this book use the equipment illustrated in this section, so to achieve the best results you should try to use the same kind of equipment.

■ STORECUPBOARD

This section tells you about useful ingredients to keep in your cupboard. You won't need them all, so buy them as you need them and you will gradually build up a useful stock.

■ TECHNIQUES

This part of the book will teach you all the basic techniques needed to create the recipes that come later. Although the Master Recipes contain cross-references to the Techniques, the Recipe Repertoire does not. If you come across an unfamiliar technique in the Repertoire look it up in the index: you will be referred either to this section or to the Master Recipes.

Look at the pictures carefully to see exactly how each step should be carried out.

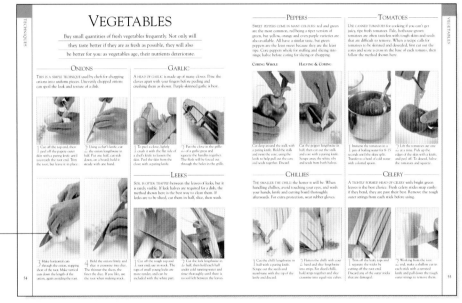

■ RECIPE REPERTOIRE

The Recipe Repertoire contains recipes that show you how to use your newly-acquired skills to create a host of classic and imaginative dishes.

—— IMPORTANT NOTES ——

■ All the weights and measurements given in this book are metric only. There is a conversion chart on page 163 if you wish to use imperial measurements but the two are not interchangeable, so use one or the other: never mix them.

■ Sometimes the recipes call for butter or oil for greasing. This is not specified in the ingredients list, so always check that you have enough before you begin.

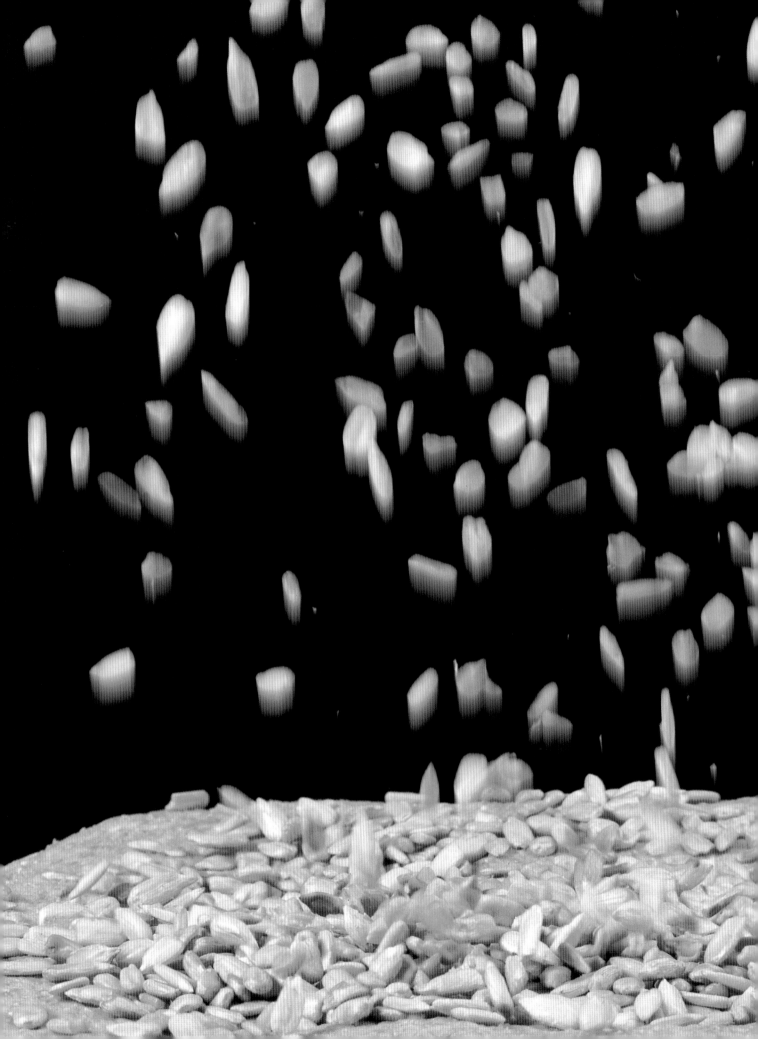

BEFORE STOCKING UP, think about the meals you are most likely to cook, then buy only those things that you know you are going to use. For storing food, use a cupboard that is in the coolest part of your kitchen – against a north-facing wall is best, but certainly not next to the radiator, boiler or oven. Make sure the cupboard is dry, and line the shelves with wipeable material. Pack the shelves logically – bags of flour together, alongside packets of rice and pasta, for example – with the things that you use most often at the front. Regularly check the use-by dates on packets, bottles and cans, and also check for foods that need to be refrigerated once opened.

STORECUPBOARD

DRY GOODS

Pasta, grains and pulses should form the backbone of your storecupboard. They keep well in a cool, dry place and provide the building blocks for an infinite variety of nutritious meals.

PASTA

DRIED PASTA KEEPS for 2 years if kept cool and dry. Authentic recipes use specific shapes, but most types are interchangeable and shape is really a matter of personal choice. Added ingredients provide colour – spinach for green pasta, tomato purée for red.

SHORT SHAPES

GNOCCHI

LUMACHE   CONCHIGLIE

Concave shell shapes, such as conchiglie, lumache, gnocchi, are good for holding chunky sauces. Giant shells can be filled with a stuffing and served with a sauce.

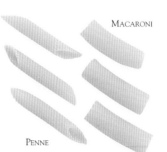

PENNE

Tubular shapes – penne, macaroni and rigatoni – are best with creamy sauces. The large, fat and ridged varieties are good for trapping chunky and meaty sauces.

MACARONI

FARFALLE

FUSILLI

Solid shapes like fusilli and farfalle are two of the most popular short pastas. They are versatile and go with most sauces, especially those made with cream or vegetables.

LONG SHAPES

Sturdy spaghetti goes with most sauces as long as any chunks of meat or fish are small; narrower spaghettini is best with light sauces. Capelli d'angelo (angel hair) is ultra-fine, so toss with ingredients that cling – olive oil, butter, pepper, grated Parmesan. Ribbons of tagliatelle are often sold coiled in nests; they are usually served with robust meat sauces.

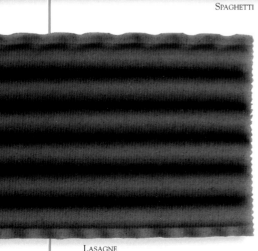

SPAGHETTI

NEST OF TAGLIATELLE

LASAGNE & CANNELLONI

Rectangular sheets of lasagne are used to make the baked dish of the same name. Best buy is the "no pre-cooking required" lasagne, which can be layered straight from the packet without boiling. Ready made cannelloni tubes are easy to fill with a stuffing when they are dry, then they are baked in a tomato or white sauce.

LASAGNE

CANNELLONI

CHINESE EGG NOODLES

These look like tangled knitting pressed into rectangular shapes, and are available in different thicknesses. Most varieties need no cooking, just soaking in hot water, so they are quick and easy to use in stir-fries and soups, and as an accompaniment to Oriental food.

FLOUR

BUY SMALL BAGS to start with, unless you plan to do a lot of baking, because most flours are best used within 6 months. Wholemeal flour should be kept for 2 months only, after which time it can become rancid.

WHITE FLOUR
Plain is traditional for thickening, batters, pastry. Self-raising is more usual for cakes, but it can be used instead of plain if it is all you have.

WHOLEMEAL FLOUR
An alternative to white flour. Has a nutty texture and flavour, and gives a heavier result. Available as plain, self-raising and strong (below left).

STRONG WHITE FLOUR
This high gluten flour is essential for making bread: if other kinds of flour are used the bread will not rise properly. Wholemeal is also available.

CORNFLOUR
Very fine white flour made from corn, for thickening liquids. Needs to be mixed to a paste with cold water before use or it will form lumps.

GRAINS

TRY ALTERNATING RICE with more unusual grains. They are easy to cook and make a pleasant change. These grains can be stored in a cool, dry place for 12 months.

WHITE LONG-GRAIN RICE
An accompaniment to, or ingredient in, savoury dishes. Grains stay separate during cooking. Sometimes labelled American rice.

EASY-COOK RICE
Alternative to white or brown rice. Grains are polished or parboiled and they never stick, so are easy to cook. Available as long and medium grain.

BROWN RICE
As for white, but longer cooking is required. Nutty flavour and rich in vitamins, minerals and protein. Long, medium and short grain.

COUSCOUS
An accompaniment to savoury dishes, especially the North African dish of the same name. Not a true grain, but a type of pasta.

BULGAR
Comes pre-boiled until the husk is cracked, then dried. Popular in the Mediterranean and Middle East, especially in pilafs and tabbouleh.

POLENTA (CORNMEAL)
A fine yellow grain made from corn or maize that is boiled in water, or boiled then grilled or fried. Widely used in Italian cooking.

PULSES

DRIED BEANS, PEAS AND LENTILS make up the family of pulses. They are easy to prepare, but all except lentils need to be soaked for at least 8 hours before boiling. They should not be kept for longer than 9 months.

RED KIDNEY BEANS
Popular in Mexican cooking, especially in chilli con carne. Their bright red skins add colour to salads and stews. Always boil rapidly for 10 minutes to get rid of toxins in the skin before cooking (see page 41).

CANNELLINI BEANS
Good general-purpose beans for soups, salads, stews and Italian cooking, especially Tuscan-style soups. They have a fluffy texture when cooked. May also be referred to as fagioli.

BLACK BEANS
Traditional in Caribbean, Mexican, Chinese and Brazilian dishes, and in American black bean soup. Their slightly sweet flavour goes particularly well with rice dishes and spicy sauces.

BORLOTTI BEANS
Very popular in Italian cooking and soups and dips because of their creamy consistency. Their streaky skins look good in mixed bean salads and casseroles. They have a slightly bittersweet flavour.

ADUKI
Good in salads, mixed with other beans, and in Chinese and Japanese rice dishes and soups. Also used in sweet dishes and as the main ingredient of red bean paste. Tender with a strong flavour when cooked.

CHICKPEAS
Most familiar in hummus, falafel and other Middle Eastern dishes, but also used in Indian curries and long-cooking Spanish casseroles. They need the longest soaking and cooking time of all the pulses.

SPLIT PEAS
Both yellow and green can be used interchangeably in soups, purées and bakes. Green split peas are sometimes served cooked to a purée and seasoned to accompany roasts and fish dishes.

LENTILS
Red or orange lentils are used for making soups, and Indian curries called dhal. They lose their shape and become mushy in consistency when cooked. Green, Puy and brown lentils keep their shape and make excellent quick vegetable side dishes.

SPICES, SEASONINGS & HERBS

Freshly ground spices are intense in flavour but quickly lose

their pungency, so buy them as you need them in small quantities and

store any leftover powder in airtight containers in the dark.

SPICES & SEEDS

SPICE SEEDS SHOULD be left whole until you are ready to use them. Dry-frying for 2–3 minutes will heighten their taste: put the seeds in a wok or frying pan and toss vigorously over high heat. You do not need to add any oil. Other seeds, particularly sesame, can be dry-fried in the same way to enhance their flavour.

CORIANDER
FLAVOUR *Highly aromatic, with a mild hint of orange peel.*
USE *Whole seeds, or ground, in Indian dishes, and with poultry, meat and vegetables, especially carrots.*

TURMERIC
FLAVOUR *Musky, peppery.*
USE *Mainly sold ground. Use to colour foods yellow, especially Indian curries and pulse dishes. Use sparingly as an alternative to saffron.*

CLOVES
FLAVOUR *Sweet, highly aromatic.*
USE *Stud onions, oranges and baked hams with whole cloves to decorate and flavour; use ground in desserts and baking, especially with fruit.*

CARDAMOM
FLAVOUR *Strong, with a lingering lemon-like aftertaste.*
USE *In Indian and Middle Eastern cooking, especially sweet dishes. Split pods and remove seeds to use.*

CUMIN
FLAVOUR *Very distinctive, slightly bitter, a little like caraway.*
USE *In Mexican, African and Indian food, and with chicken and vegetables. Difficult to crush at home.*

CINNAMON
FLAVOUR *Subtle, spicy-sweet.*
USE *Ground when poaching fruit, and in pies, cakes and biscuits. Infuse sticks in sugar syrups, milk and custards and mulled wines.*

GINGER
FLAVOUR *Hot, pungent, warming.*
USE *In desserts and baking, pickles and chutneys, and in Indian and Chinese spice mixtures. Can be used as a substitute for fresh root ginger.*

SAFFRON
FLAVOUR *Pungent, aromatic, sometimes faintly bitter.*
USE *Traditionally a very highly sought-after spice, made from the dried stigmas of certain crocus flowers. Used for colouring foods yellow, especially rice and fish dishes, sweet breads and biscuits. Soak threads in warm water for 20 minutes, strain and use liquid. Alternatively, sprinkle powder directly into liquids and stir to avoid streaking.*

MACE

NUTMEG
FLAVOUR *Sweet, warm, quite powerful. More pungent if grated fresh whenever it is needed, preferably at the end of cooking.*
USE *In sweet dishes, in savoury sauces and with vegetables.*
Mace, more expensive and more refined in flavour than nutmeg, is the lacy outer covering. Use to infuse sauces and soups, shellfish and cheese dishes. Like the nutmeg itself, this is available either whole – pressed flat and dried – or ground.

CARAWAY SEEDS
FLAVOUR *Pungent, bittersweet.*
USE *In Austrian and German soups, stews, vegetable dishes; in breads and biscuits, especially Jewish recipes. Good with cheese, pork, sausages.*

WHITE SESAME SEEDS
FLAVOUR *Mildly nutty, best recognized in tahini paste made from ground white sesame seeds.*
USE *In Middle Eastern and Chinese cooking. Often used toasted.*

POPPY SEEDS
FLAVOUR *Nutty, slightly sweet.*
USE *In baking and Indian dishes, as a garnish for salads, noodles and vegetables. Grey-blue seeds are most common. Can be used toasted.*

DILL SEEDS
FLAVOUR *Lingering, with a hint of aniseed similar to caraway.*
USE *In Scandinavian and Eastern European cooking with fish, pickled cucumber, vegetables. Also in breads.*

THE PEPPER FAMILY

MANY PEPPERS are made from dried capsicums. These are different from everyday pepper, which is ground from peppercorns. Different pepper products vary in heat, so it is wise to know which is which.

PAPRIKA
FLAVOUR *The mildest of the pepper family. Available in sweet (mild) and hot forms. Sweet is most useful.*
USE *In Hungarian and Spanish dishes, and as a colourful garnish.*

CAYENNE
FLAVOUR *Made from one of the hottest varieties of chillies.*
USE *In Mexican and Cajun dishes, and to add piquancy and heat to other foods according to taste.*

DRIED CHILLIES

CHILLI FLAKES
FLAVOUR *Very fiery with lots of chilli seeds, so use with caution.*
USE *Sprinkle sparingly in or over foods, before or after cooking. Make it yourself at home by crushing dried red chillies in a pestle and mortar.*

CHILLI POWDER
FLAVOUR *In fact a blend of chillies, garlic, cumin and oregano. Different brands will vary in heat.*
USE *For authentic Mexican, Indian and southwest American dishes.*

SPICE MIXTURES

READY-MADE blends of ground spices are time-saving, economical, and very handy to have in the storecupboard. The choice is vast, and mixtures vary according to individual manufacturers and brands. The three shown here are the most commonly used.

CURRY POWDER
FLAVOUR *Varies from Indian through Chinese to Thai, some perfumed and mild, others hot.*
USE *Gives curries an authentic flavour, which is often difficult to achieve by mixing spices yourself.*

GARAM MASALA
FLAVOUR *Usually a mix of cumin, coriander, cardamom, cloves, cinnamon, pepper, mace and bay.*
USE *In curries, particularly North Indian, which are mild and perfumed rather than fiery and hot.*

MIXED SPICE
FLAVOUR *Traditional English mixture of six ground sweet spices, usually allspice, cinnamon, cloves, coriander, mace and nutmeg.*
USE *Mainly in puddings and desserts, cakes and biscuits.*

SALT & PEPPER

THESE ARE ESSENTIAL in the storecupboard, both for cooking and as table condiments. There are many different types – these are the most useful.

TABLE SALT
TYPE *Refined rock salt with anti-caking agents. Free-flowing.*
USE *For cooking and at the table. Better than the less refined kitchen or cooking salt, which tends to clog, and is not fine enough for table use.*

COARSE SALT
TYPE *Large or medium-size crystals. Choose from rock or sea salt; sea salt tastes slightly stronger.*
USE *For cooking and at the table. A salt mill is often used to grind large crystals, but this is not essential.*

BLACK PEPPER
TYPE *Whole peppercorns and ready-ground black pepper.*
USE *For freshness, grind peppercorns in a pepper mill when you need them. Ready-ground is useful for seasoning large quantities of food.*

MIXED PEPPERCORNS
TYPE *A blend of whole black, white, pink, green peppercorns. Five-pepper blends include allspice berries.*
USE *For grinding in or over food. A spicy and attractive alternative to black or white peppercorns.*

DRIED HERBS

FRESH HERBS are preferable to dried in salads and sauces, but dried herbs are often better in dishes like casseroles and stews that require long cooking, so a small stock of dried herbs is essential.

Freeze-dried herbs have a good aroma, colour and flavour, but their flavour is generally concentrated, so use half the quantity of dried to fresh. To store, keep them in airtight containers in the dark, or at least away from sunlight. Aroma and flavour should stay fresh for up to 12 months.

SAGE
FLAVOUR *Slightly bitter, stronger than fresh sage.*
USE *Good with meat, especially fatty pork, duck and sausages, and with veal and offal. Also good in cooked egg and cheese dishes. Use sparingly.*

DILL
FLAVOUR *Subtle, tones of aniseed. Less pungent than fresh.*
USE *For marinades and dressings, especially in Northern and Eastern European cooking with cucumber, fish and root vegetables.*

OREGANO
FLAVOUR *Powerful, almost spicy. A variety of wild marjoram.*
USE *In Mediterranean and Italian dishes – with tomatoes, in pasta sauces and on pizza. Also frequently used in Mexican cooking.*

BAY
FLAVOUR *Pungent, resinous; stronger if leaves are torn before use. Long cooking releases flavour best.*
USE *In stocks, sauces, soups and stews. For infusing milk and in bouquet garni. Also good with fish.*

MIXED HERBS
FLAVOUR *Usually a mixture of marjoram, oregano, rosemary, summer savory and thyme.*
USE *In sauces and stews, cooked tomato dishes, sprinkled over pizza. Can be used in most savoury dishes.*

BASIL
FLAVOUR *Sweet, spicy. Slightly more minty than fresh basil.*
USE *In salads and long-cooking Mediterranean sauces and casseroles, especially with tomatoes. Traditionally partnered with garlic.*

ROSEMARY
FLAVOUR *Pungent, spicy yet refreshing. Milder than fresh rosemary.*
USE *In casseroles and marinades with lamb, pork, chicken, and with potatoes. Used in Italian dishes, and to flavour bread, such as focaccia.*

OILS & VINEGARS

Rows of different bottles of glistening oils and vinegars make a
spectacular display, but only a few of the more versatile types are
really necessary to bring out the best in your cooking.

OILS

USED FOR FRYING, brushing, basting, marinades and
dressings, oils are made from vegetables, fruit, nuts or
seeds and are healthier than animal fats. Store in a cool
place and check labels for storage times – they vary.

VINEGARS

BOTTLED VINEGARS ARE A GOOD BUY, but don't display
them on the kitchen windowsill or they will quickly lose
their flavour. Store somewhere cold and dark, and they
will taste good for up to 2 years.

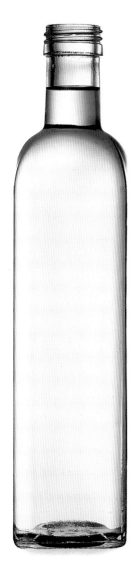    

SUNFLOWER OIL
FLAVOUR *Very light and
neutral, virtually tasteless.*
USE *General-purpose oil
that can be used for all
cooking purposes. Good
mixed half and half with
olive oil for extra flavour.*

OLIVE OIL
FLAVOUR *Mildly fruity, but
brands vary. "Virgin" is
good as it has a low acidity
level and is less refined.*
USE *In Mediterranean
dishes, marinades, grilling,
barbecuing, shallow frying.*

EXTRA VIRGIN OLIVE OIL
FLAVOUR *Peppery, fruity.
From the first cold pressing.*
USE *For dressing salads
and cold dishes, and
sprinkling over hot foods
just before serving.*

WINE VINEGAR
FLAVOUR *Red and white
are mildly fruity, sherry is
nutty and brown. Balsamic
is oak-matured and musky.*
USE *In dressings, sauces
and marinades. Use less of
balsamic – it is strong.*

CIDER VINEGAR
FLAVOUR *Strong, like a
sharp cider.*
USE *As wine vinegar, but
has a stronger taste so use
less. Use with pork, offal,
sausages, and in pickles,
chutneys and dressings.*

BOTTLED & PRESERVED FOOD

For use at the table and as quick-and-easy instant flavourings, bottled sauces and preserves are well worth stocking. Check labels for storage directions – some need to be kept in the refrigerator once opened.

SAUCES & PRESERVES

ADD A DASH of soy sauce, a drop of Tabasco or a spoonful of ketchup, and the flavour of a dish can be transformed. There is a huge variety of sauces and preserves on the market, and it is a matter of personal taste which you choose to keep in stock.

TABASCO SAUCE
FLAVOUR *Fiery hot, made from a secret recipe based on chillies.*
USE *In Mexican cooking, and to give a kick to any bland food.*

HORSERADISH SAUCE
FLAVOUR *Pungent, hot horseradish root with vinegar and cream.*
USE *With beef, cold meats, smoked fish, chicken and eggs.*

WORCESTERSHIRE SAUCE
FLAVOUR *Piquant, salty, with anchovies, molasses, tamarind.*
USE *To spice up bland foods, sauces, marinades, dressings.*

TOMATO KETCHUP
FLAVOUR *Unique blend of tomatoes, vinegar and sugar.*
USE *In marinades, dressings, stews, sauces and relishes.*

SOY SAUCE
FLAVOUR *Chinese light soy is mild; dark is strong and salty. Japanese soy is less salty, slightly sweet.*
USE *In Oriental dishes, stir-fries.*

MANGO CHUTNEY
FLAVOUR *Fruity, sweet, with chunks of mango. Some are hot and spicy.*
USE *In Indian dishes, dressings, sauces. With cheese, mayonnaise.*

REDCURRANT JELLY
FLAVOUR *Very sweet.*
USE *To add sweetness and colour to gravies and sauces, especially with pork, poultry and game.*

MUSTARD

MADE FROM THE SEEDS of the mustard plant, mustard appears in many different flavours, colours and textures. Everyone has their own favourites, and any of them can be used in cooking or as a condiment. The three shown here provide a good contrast in flavours and textures.

DIJON
FLAVOUR *Strong, made from the hottest mustard seeds.*
USE *In sauces, dips, dressings, mayonnaise and marinades.*

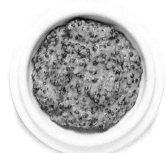

COARSE-GRAIN
FLAVOUR *Usually mild, but some types are hot. Sometimes vinegary.*
USE *As for Dijon, for a milder flavour and crunchier texture.*

ENGLISH
FLAVOUR *Very hot, pungent.*
USE *Add powder to sauces, dips, marinades. Or mix to a paste with cold water and use as for Dijon.*

TOMATOES

FRESH TOMATOES are always available, but often lack flavour. Whole or chopped canned tomatoes in natural juice taste good all year round and make a good substitute. These tomato-based products are also useful for adding richness and depth.

SUN-DRIED TOMATOES IN OIL
TYPE *Halves or pieces, packed in olive oil in jars or sold loose.*
USE *In salads, sauces and stews.*

CONCENTRATES
TYPE *Purée and paste. Sun-dried paste has a mellow, sweet flavour.*
USE *For flavouring, colouring and thickening sauces, soups and stews.*

PASSATA
TYPE *Sieved crushed tomatoes in cans and bottles.*
USE *In sauces, soups and stews; for a smooth, thick consistency.*

DESSERTS & BAKING ESSENTIALS

SWEETENERS

WHITE SUGAR
Caster is best for cooking – it is fine and dissolves quickly; granulated is coarse, and is best for table use.

ICING SUGAR
Powdered refined sugar for icings and sweet sauces. Also for sifting over desserts, pies and cakes for decorative effect.

MAPLE SYRUP
Use in ice-cream, cakes and biscuits, also to pour over pancakes and waffles. Flavour is more distinctive than golden syrup.

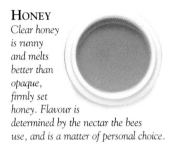

SOFT BROWN SUGAR
Light and dark; both are refined, with molasses added. Use instead of white sugar for colour and flavour, especially in baked goods.

DEMERARA SUGAR
Crunchy raw sugar. Crystals do not dissolve easily, but give good texture if sprinkled on top of desserts, cakes and biscuits before baking.

HONEY
Clear honey is runny and melts better than opaque, firmly set honey. Flavour is determined by the nectar the bees use, and is a matter of personal choice.

RAISING & SETTING AGENTS

FAST-ACTION YEAST
A powder that mixes directly into flour. Quicker and more convenient to use than other types of yeast.

BAKING POWDER
Leavening agent used in cakes and biscuits. A mixture of bicarbonate of soda, sodium and cream of tartar.

BICARBONATE OF SODA
Used as a raising agent combined with an acid such as sour milk.

GELATINE POWDER
A setting agent that must be dissolved in liquid before use. Sachets are most convenient. Not for vegetarians.

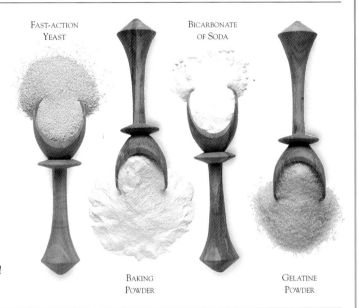

FAST-ACTION YEAST

BICARBONATE OF SODA

BAKING POWDER

GELATINE POWDER

FLAVOURINGS

EXTRACTS
For best flavour, always buy pure extracts, not synthetic essences. Vanilla and almond are most useful.

CHOCOLATE
For the most chocolatey flavour, buy good-quality chocolate with a minimum of 70 per cent cocoa solids.

COCOA POWDER
Instant chocolate flavour for cakes, sauces and desserts. Saves melting.

VANILLA PODS
For infusing custards with pure vanilla flavour. Split lengthwise before use. Can be stored in a jar of sugar to make vanilla sugar.

VANILLA PODS

VANILLA EXTRACT   ALMOND EXTRACT

CHOCOLATE   COCOA POWDER

19

BUY THE BEST equipment you can afford –
it is false economy to save money at the
outset because cheap equipment simply
will not last. Good equipment will make
preparation of ingredients and cooking
easier for you, and it will also save you
time. Think hard about the equipment
you will need to start with, and buy the
bare minimum, then collect more pieces
as and when you need them, gradually
building up a *batterie de cuisine*. This will
spread the cost, and prevent your kitchen
cupboard and work surface being
cluttered up with things you don't use.

EQUIPMENT

KNIVES & GADGETS

A selection of carefully chosen knives is essential in the kitchen.

Gadgets are useful but take up valuable storage space, so

buy as the need arises and build up a set that suits your cooking style.

KNIVES

BUY GOOD-QUALITY knives and keep them in a block or on a wall-mounted magnetic strip: knives kept in a drawer go blunt quickly and are a danger to fingers reaching in.

SERRATED KNIFE
This 8cm knife blade is for slicing, especially vegetables such as tomatoes that are firm outside and soft inside.

PARING KNIFE
A knife for fine work, such as peeling (paring), and cutting cores from apple quarters and peppers. The blade is 10cm long.

CHEF'S KNIFE
All-purpose chopping knife with a 19cm blade: keep the tip on the board and rock the handle up and down, moving the blade across the food.

BREAD KNIFE
A serrated knife with a 21cm blade will penetrate bread crusts cleanly. Serrated knives cannot be sharpened.

 SAFETY PRONG

CARVING FORK
Holds the meat firmly. Safety prong prevents the knife blade from slipping towards the carver.

CARVING KNIFE
This 19cm, thin, flexible blade is perfect for carving meat in thin slices. The knife should curve upwards towards the tip.

SHARPENING STEEL
To keep knives sharp, draw the blade lightly down the steel at a shallow angle. Repeat several times to the front and back of the steel.

 SAFETY GUARD

BOARDS
Wooden boards are kindest to knives. Keep different boards for different purposes so there is no possibility of raw food contaminating cooked food. Clean thoroughly after use.

KNIFE SHARPENER
Easier for the beginner to use than a steel. Draw the blade backwards through the sharpener several times, keeping the knife upright.

SWIVEL PEELER
The handle of this peeler is easy to grip and the rocking blade slides over the contours of the most knobbly vegetable. The hardened steel blade will stay sharp, but can rust, so dry well after washing.

CAN OPENER
A sturdy, well-made can opener will work easily and leave no dangerous jagged edges. Look for cutting wheels like these and handles that are comfortable to hold.

APPLE CORER
Comes into its own when stuffing apples for baking, or making apple rings when you want to keep apples whole but remove the cores cleanly.

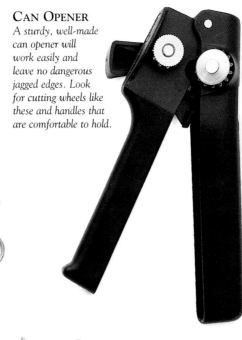

SKEWERS
Use a flat-bladed skewer so that when you turn a kebab over the food turns over with it.

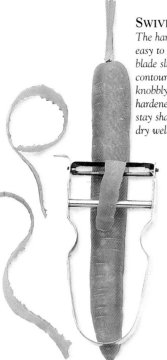

LARGE PALETTE KNIFE
This knife is used for spreading, not cutting, and has a flat, blunt, highly flexible 21cm blade. Use it to coat a cake evenly with jam or icing, or to layer white sauce in a lasagne.

ZESTER
Use to get pure strips of citrus zest (oil-rich rind with no white pith). Choose a sturdy one with a comfortable handle as you will have to grip quite hard to get the required result.

CORKSCREW
This corkscrew is easier to use than most other kinds: it only requires a single action to withdraw the cork.

SCISSORS
Keep a pair solely for kitchen use. They are perfect for trimming rind off bacon, snipping herbs, and other small tasks.

BOTTLE STOPPER
To preserve wine or soft drinks once the bottle has been opened.

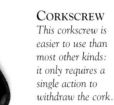

SMALL PALETTE KNIFE
Immensely useful for all spreading tasks, but especially for softened butter; also good for loosening a cake's edges from its tin.

BOTTLE OPENER
Choose a simple, sturdy bottle opener with a handle that is easy to grip.

23

PROCESSING TOOLS

It is essential to use the right tool for the job – a cliché, but

a concept that is very important in the kitchen. The

wrong tools will only cause frustration and waste valuable time.

PROCESSING BY HAND

GOOD INGREDIENTS deserve good treatment. Having the right processing tools means wasting less of the food you buy. These are the basic items that every cook should have.

BOX GRATER
Better than a flat grater because it stands up. Remember to shake grated ingredients out before they get too compressed. Two grating surfaces (large and small holes) suffice.

POTATO MASHER
It takes effort to mash potatoes so choose a masher with a comfortable handle, such as this rubber one.

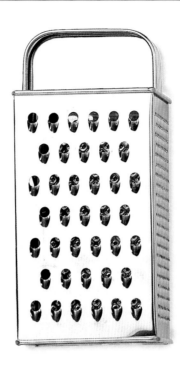

PESTLE & MORTAR
Buy the biggest one you can easily store. Porcelain is a good choice as it has the weight of marble without the prohibitive cost.

PEPPER & SALT MILLS
Freshly ground pepper is a must. Pepper loses its aroma soon after crushing, so ready-ground is a bad buy. The salt mill makes up the pair: it uses large crystals of rock or sea salt.

NUTMEG GRATER
As with pepper, so with nutmeg – always grind your own as and when you need it. There is a compartment in the top to store the whole nutmeg.

LEMON SQUEEZER
This rigid plastic squeezer has a bowl to catch all the lemon juice and a well-fitting strainer to keep the pips out.

DETACHABLE GRILLE

GARLIC PRESS
Choose a sturdy, all-metal press with a detachable grille to make cleaning easy.

24

PROCESSING BY MACHINE

EQUIPPING YOUR KITCHEN with the full range of electric machines is costly and wastes storage space. When buying, think carefully about what you cook, how often and the quantities involved.

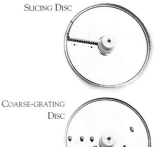

SLICING DISC

COARSE-GRATING DISC

FINE-GRATING DISC

CHIPPER DISC

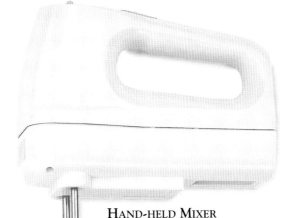

HAND-HELD MIXER

Much faster than whisking and mixing by hand. Leaves you with one hand free and can be used in a pan over the heat. Choose one with three speeds and beaters that are easy to remove for cleaning.

BLENDER

Also called liquidizer. Use to purée foods for soups, dips, batters and drinks. Look for a model with blades set low to cope with small quantities.

FOOD PROCESSOR

Eliminates the need for a free-standing blender. The metal blade chops and mixes, attachment discs shred and grate. The more expensive the processor, the more sophisticated the jobs it will do. Some come with a mini bowl for processing small quantities.

MINI BOWL

HAND-HELD BLENDER

Use to purée foods in the pan. Less expensive, more portable version of the liquidizer; it saves on washing up and storage space. A handy item for small quantities – it may be all you need.

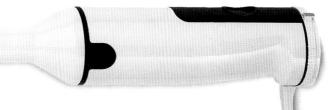

MEASURING & MIXING

Never underestimate the need for accurate measurements,

especially when baking. Using the right tools for

sieving and mixing ingredients is critical for the end result too.

MEASURING

BUYING AND USING good measuring equipment will always pay off, especially when it comes to baking pies, bread or cakes, when accuracy is so important for successful results.

MEASURING JUG
Buy the biggest you can store: a large jug is more versatile, and useful for mixing. Plastic is safer and longer-lasting than glass, but glass is better for hot liquids. A good jug will have both metric and imperial measurements to help with converting quantities.

CUPS
In American recipes, solids and liquids are both measured by volume. The standard measure is the cup, which holds 250ml or 8fl oz (an American pint is 16fl oz; an English pint is 20fl oz). Shown here are 1 cup, ½ cup, ⅓ cup and ¼ cup measures.

MIXING & SIEVING

THE WOODEN SPOON is often used as a symbol of good home cooking. Certainly it does plenty of work, but the spatula and the cornered spoon are probably more versatile.

SPOONS
When a recipe calls for teaspoons and tablespoons, these should be level – and measured accurately. Invest in a commercially produced set; ordinary spoons are not accurate enough.

SCALES
Balance scales such as these give the most accurate results, especially for small amounts. Choose a set of metric weights: the large weights are usually iron, the smaller ones brass.

WOODEN SPOONS
A short-handled wooden spoon is useful for mixing and beating by hand. Long-handled spoons are good for stirring mixtures on the stove. They stand up to the heat (without burning your hand) and do not scratch the pan. A spoon with a corner will reach right to the edges at the base of a pan.

SIEVES

It is handy to have two: large and small. Besides sifting dry ingredients and straining wet ones, you can use a sieve to purée cooked fruit and vegetables, and to make puréed soups.

LADLE

SERVING SPOON

SLOTTED SPOON

FISH SLICE

COLANDER

Choose a free-standing, sturdy colander with handles for safe draining of cooked vegetables, pasta and pulses.

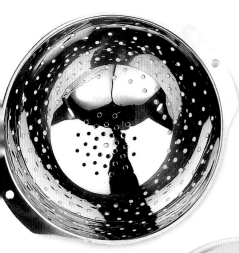

BOWLS

Useful to have plenty of sizes, but choose ones that fit inside each other so that they do not take up all your storage space. Glass is versatile, and gives you an all-round view of what you are mixing.

KITCHEN TOOL SET

Ladle *To avoid pouring hot liquids from heavy pans, use this for serving soups and stews.*

Serving spoon *The handle gets hot if this spoon is left in the pan, so use for serving only.*

Fish slice *For any solid food that needs turning in the pan or lifting carefully from pan to plate. It is especially useful for delicate foods like fish that have a tendency to break up.*

Slotted spoon *Invaluable when removing food from boiling water for serving or testing, and for skimming scum from the surface of liquids. Can be either round or spoon-shaped.*

WOODEN SPATULA

This flat-sided spatula is used for folding mixtures, like egg whites or melted chocolate and cake mixture, together. It doubles up as a lifter and turner too.

BALLOON WHISK

A comfortable handle and a large balloon of springy wire will make light work of whisking egg whites if you don't have an electric whisk. A good tool to use whenever you need to incorporate air into a mixture.

COIL WHISK

Ideal for whisking small quantities of sauce over the heat or in a roasting tin – but do not use on nonstick finishes.

PLASTIC SPATULA

A flexible spatula is the best way to make sure you get every last bit of mixture out of the bowl. Like a wooden spatula, it is good for folding mixtures too.

TONGS

Useful for turning and moving delicate pieces of hot food, for example when char-grilling.

PASTRY TOOLS

PASTRY-MAKING IS A PRECISE ART, and you will need some special tools besides cold hands if you are going to be successful. You can either make the pastry on a board (see page 22) or work directly on a floured work surface – marble is ideal because it stays cool.

PASTRY BRUSH

Use for sealing and glazing. This is the flat, paintbrush kind – easier to use than the round type.

PIE FUNNEL

Holds up the pastry lid, and pokes through the top so that steam can escape and the pastry stays crisp.

PASTRY CUTTERS

Available plain and fluted as shown here, and also in a wide range of shapes and sizes, from letters of the alphabet to hearts and stars.

WOODEN ROLLING PIN

Choose a heavy, smooth rolling pin without handles. The best way to roll pastry is to roll the whole pin under the palms, sliding the hands up and down to distribute the weight evenly – handles are not necessary.

BAKING BEANS

For baking pastry blind. You can use rice or pulses, but ceramic ones are heavier and more effective.

POTS & PANS

Pans are perhaps the most important pieces of equipment in your kitchen, so buy the best you can afford. Choose quality pans and they will last for years, and save you wasting time and burning food.

CHOOSING PANS

YOU NEED A MINIMUM of three deep pans and one shallow pan. A sauté pan is the most versatile of the shallow pans. Unless otherwise stated, measurements are taken across the top.

STEAMER BASKET
A collapsible steamer basket stands on metal legs inside the pan. It can be folded up when not in use and is less expensive than a proper steamer.

LARGE PAN
Like the medium pan, this 22cm version also doubles up as a casserole. It holds almost 5 litres and can be used to hold a steamer basket.

MEDIUM PAN
This 18cm two-handled pan can be used on the stove and in the oven: its two short metal handles allow it to fit in the oven like a casserole dish. It holds 2.5 litres, a useful size for most cooking purposes, and comes with a tight-fitting lid.

SAUCEPAN
This 16cm pan holds 2 litres. It has a multitude of uses, from sauces and vegetables to soups and small stews. A long handle will stay cool on a hot hob.

MILK PAN
Holds almost 1 litre of liquid. Nonstick is best for sauces with milk or cream in them because they have a tendency to stick. Pouring lips on both sides make serving easier. Nonstick finishes vary widely and never last for ever: the better the quality the more durable they will be.

OMELETTE PAN
A pan with a nonstick finish is easiest to use, even though chefs prefer cast iron or stainless steel. The right size is important: measuring across the base, use a 16cm pan for a 2-egg French omelette, a 23cm pan for a thick Spanish or Italian omelette. These pans are also useful for making pancakes.

WOK

Choose a large wok (35cm across the top) if you have room to store it. Pre-seasoned carbon steel is easy to care for and can take metal implements; unseasoned carbon steel rusts more easily. A wok with a slightly flattened bottom is most stable on both gas and electric hobs. Woks often come complete with ladle, spatula and shovel.

SHOVEL

SPATULA

WOK LID

LADLE

SAUTÉ PAN

A good-quality, nonstick 20cm sauté pan will prove useful for shallow frying as well as boiling or stir-frying. A sauté pan has deeper, straighter sides than a frying pan. This one has a removable handle, which, like the short-handled pans on the facing page, allows for oven use. The glass lid enables you to see what is happening when you cover the pan.

CHAR-GRILL PAN

Cooking in a ridged pan on the hob is an easy way to achieve a professional-looking char-grilled result at home. Choose a pan that has well-defined ridges, and is not too heavy to lift. A foldaway handle is useful for easy storage.

CHOICE OF MATERIALS FOR PANS

STAINLESS STEEL IS THE BEST ALL-ROUND CHOICE: extremely durable and easy to clean. For the best heat conduction, buy good-quality pans that have heavy bases made of a sandwich of stainless steel with a metal filling. Good conductors of heat are copper, copper and silver alloy or aluminium, so look for one of these fillings. Although they are expensive, they should last a very long time.

29

BAKING & ROASTING

Equipment for baking and roasting is probably not used every day, so you need not spend a fortune. However, avoid anything flimsy. Tins that flex in the hands may cast your handiwork on the floor.

OVENWARE

THE CHOICE OF METAL or ceramic, nonstick or uncoated, depends largely on the job you want the equipment to do. Whatever you buy, look after it carefully to avoid rusting and scratching.

SANDWICH TIN
This loose-bottomed cake tin is 18cm in diameter and shallow. You will need two to make a Victoria sandwich, but you may like to invest in more if you make a lot of layered cakes. A nonstick coating is not necessary.

RAMEKINS
Ramekins – small ceramic baking dishes – are for individual servings of soufflés and baked custards, and can be brought straight to the table from the oven. Buy them as and when needed. Average capacity is 150ml.

YORKSHIRE PUDDING AND MUFFIN TIN

MUFFIN TIN
A nonstick coating is useful in a muffin and Yorkshire pudding tin. Otherwise, use paper cases for muffins and grease the tin well when making individual Yorkshire puddings.

BAKING SHEET
Buy the largest one that will fit comfortably in your oven. It should be sturdy, inflexible and completely flat. Use it for pizzas and cookies, and to provide a heat-conducting base for quiches, pies and tarts.

COOLING RACK
Cakes should always be cooled before being filled, sandwiched together or iced, and a metal cooling rack allows air to circulate around them.

COOLING RACK

SPRINGFORM CAKE TIN
This is 20cm in diameter. The clasp on the side opens the tin and releases the bottom, so a cake can be removed easily. Use a tin of this size and style for delicate cakes and cheesecakes that break up easily. Nonstick is not necessary: a cake tin needs to be lined and greased for a good result whatever the material it is made from or its coating.

TRAYBAKE TIN
A deep-sided tray, measuring 30 x 23cm across the top. Take care not to scratch the nonstick surface.

LOAF TIN
A 20 x 10cm nonstick tin is a good size for bread, cakes, pâtés and terrines.

BAKING SHEET

TRAYBAKE TIN

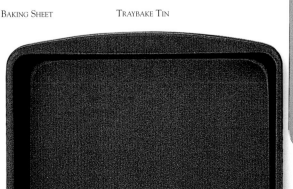

BAKING DISH
A well-made ceramic dish measuring 25 x 20cm across the top and 5cm in depth is perfect for baked pasta dishes, and can be used for roasting as well. Dishes such as these cannot usually bear sudden and extreme temperature changes: while they are fine in the oven, they must not be transferred to a hob. Nor should cold water be poured into a very hot dish to cool it down: it might crack.

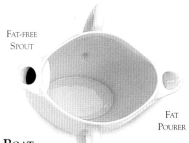

FAT-FREE SPOUT

FAT POURER

FRENCH GRAVY BOAT
This gravy boat enables the diner to pour fat-free gravies and sauces. Fat, being light, floats to the surface and can be poured off through a shallow spout. The deep spout reaches into the liquid below.

PIE TIN
Metal is better than ceramic or ovenproof glass for cooking pastry because it distributes the heat more evenly and gives a crisper result. A very hot baking sheet under the pie tin increases heat conduction. Pie tins have plain, sloping sides and a lip for the pie edging. A good all-purpose size is 23cm across the top.

POULTRY PINS
Small pins can be used to truss poultry to hold it together while it cooks.

ROASTING TIN
Best of all is a deep, enamelled tray with a pouring lip. It should be strong, rigid, and as big as your oven will take.

MEAT THERMOMETER
Use for large birds and joints of meat: insert the thermometer probe through the thickest part of the meat at the start of cooking. For temperatures, see page 160.

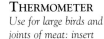

ROASTING RACK
A rack enables meat to be roasted free of its own fat. A hinged one can be folded to cradle a bird.

QUICHE TIN
As with the pie tin above, a metal quiche tin performs better than a ceramic one. Quiches are fragile, and the fluted edge helps strengthen the pastry shell. This tin measures 20cm across the base, which lifts out so the whole quiche can be removed without breaking. For easy serving, leave the quiche on the base.

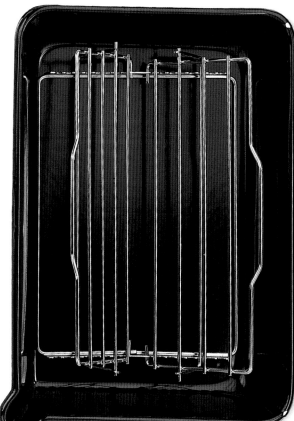

USING AN OVEN

FEW NEW COOKS HAVE THE LUXURY OF CHOOSING their own oven, but whatever is available, each oven will vary in performance: the only way to know an oven's quirks is to use it. Adjust temperatures and cooking times to suit your oven. Fan ovens are hotter than conventional ovens, so lower temperatures are given, but always consult the manufacturer's handbook.

POURING LIP

GOOD BASIC COOKING SKILLS are essential for the new cook, and they're easy to master. Once you've learnt them, you will never forget them, and you will be confident that you can cook well and have successful results every time. In this chapter you will learn how to choose ingredients wisely and how to prepare them correctly. You will also learn basic cooking methods; the ones you will use over and over again on a daily basis. Step-by-step photographs guide you effortlessly through, from simple skills like cracking an egg without breaking the yolk, to boiling potatoes and cooking spaghetti, and more tricky tasks like stuffing and trussing a turkey.

TECHNIQUES

EGGS

Eggs are one of the cheapest sources of complete protein and could

not be easier to cook. Once you have mastered these simple

techniques you will be able to produce a nutritious meal in minutes.

BOILING

REMOVE EGGS FROM THE REFRIGERATOR 30 minutes before cooking: if they are very cold, they will crack in hot water. Timings given here are for large eggs. For safety information on soft-boiled eggs, see page 162.

SOFT BOILING

Using a slotted spoon, gently lower the egg into a small saucepan two-thirds full of simmering water. Bring to the boil, lower the heat to a gentle simmer and set a timer for 4 minutes. When the time is up, remove the egg with a slotted spoon, and slice across the top with a knife. The egg will have a runny yolk.

HARD BOILING

Follow the instructions for soft boiling, but simmer the egg for 10 minutes. Do not boil for longer or a black ring will form around the yolk. Lift the egg out with a slotted spoon and plunge it into a bowl of cold water. Crack the shell and peel it off. Immerse the egg in cold water for at least 5 minutes until cool.

CRACKING AN EGG

THERE IS NO SPECIAL TRICK to prevent egg yolks from breaking when you crack open the shell, so always crack each egg into an empty bowl.

Tap the middle of the egg sharply against the rim of a small bowl. Holding the egg low over the bowl, insert the tips of your thumbs into the crack in the shell and gently prise the egg apart. Tip the contents of the egg into the bowl and discard the shell. Remove any pieces of shell with the tip of a teaspoon.

FRYING

ALWAYS ENSURE that the fat is hot before adding the egg. If you like a yolk with a film of white on top, continue spooning the fat over it in step 2 until it is opaque. For safety information on runny yolks, see page 162.

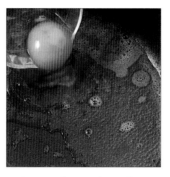

1 Heat 1 tbsp each sunflower oil and butter in a sauté pan until foaming. Slide the egg from a bowl into the pan.

2 Fry over medium heat for 3–4 minutes until the white is set, spooning the fat over the yolk to help it cook.

3 Lift the egg out with a fish slice and let the fat drain back into the pan. If frying more than 1 egg, cut the whites apart with the fish slice first.

Poaching

USE EITHER A NONSTICK MILK PAN or sauté pan. Fill the pan two-thirds full with water and bring to the boil, then add a pinch of salt. Turn the heat down so the water is simmering gently before adding the eggs: rapidly boiling water will break up the whites. A nonstick egg poacher that cooks eggs in butter can also be used. For safety information on softly poached eggs, see page 162.

Scrambling

EGGS ARE BEST SCRAMBLED in a nonstick pan, such as a milk or sauté pan, so they do not stick and burn on the bottom. For creamy scrambled eggs, the secret is to cook the eggs very gently and slowly, stirring all the time. Serve plain or with chopped fresh herbs. For a special occasion, replace the milk with cream and serve the eggs scattered with thin strips of smoked salmon.

  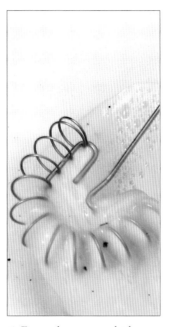 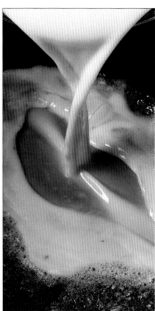

1 Slide the egg from a bowl into gently simmering salted water. Turn the heat down to low.

2 Poach, uncovered, over low heat for about 3 minutes until the white is opaque and the yolk is runny.

1 For each person, whisk together 2 eggs, 1 tbsp milk and a little salt and pepper.

2 Heat 1 tbsp butter in the pan until foaming, then pour in the egg mixture.

3 Lift the egg out with a slotted spoon and let the excess water drain back into the pan.

3 Cook over low heat, stirring gently with a wooden spatula. When almost set, remove from the heat, stir for 1 more minute, then serve at once.

EGGS

SEPARATING EGGS

IF YOU NEED EGG WHITES for soufflés or meringues, or yolks for mayonnaise, you must separate the whites from the yolks before you start. For 1 egg, use two bowls: one for the white and one for the yolk. If separating more eggs, use three bowls and separate over an empty bowl each time, tipping the whites and yolks into separate bowls.

Tap the middle of the egg sharply against the rim of a small bowl. Hold the egg low over the bowl and prise the shell apart with the tips of your thumbs. Tilt gently to pour the white into the bowl while retaining the yolk in the shell. Tip the yolk from the shell into the second bowl.

WHISKING EGG WHITES

YOU WILL GET a greater volume when whisking egg whites if they are at room temperature rather than cold, so take them out of the refrigerator 30 minutes before needed. Equipment must be scrupulously clean and dry.

1 Place the egg whites in a large bowl. Using an electric mixer on full speed, begin whisking, moving the beaters around the bowl.

2 Continue whisking on full speed, still moving the beaters around the bowl, until the egg whites stand in stiff peaks. Use at once.

MAKING MERINGUES

THIS RECIPE makes 12 meringues. They are usually sandwiched in pairs. For serving ideas, see page 152.

INGREDIENTS

2 egg whites

110g caster sugar

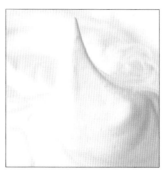

1 Preheat the oven to 140°C (fan oven 120°C), Gas 1. Whisk the whites until stiff (see left), then add the sugar 1 tsp at a time, whisking on full speed until glossy.

2 Cover a baking sheet with a piece of nonstick baking parchment. Place 12 individual dessertspoonfuls of the mixture on to the paper, swirling them with the back of the spoon.

3 Bake for ¾–1 hour until firm and crisp. Lift one to check that it comes easily off the paper. Leave the meringues to cool slightly, then lift them off with a fish slice.

MAKING PANCAKE BATTER

VERY THIN PANCAKES, called *crêpes* in French, are quite tricky to make because they tend to stick and tear, so it is easier to make fewer, thicker pancakes the first few times you try. It is not essential to let the batter stand.

INGREDIENTS

| 125g plain flour |
| 2 eggs |
| 250ml milk, either full cream or semi-skimmed |

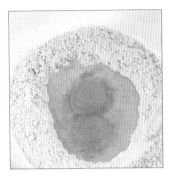

1 Measure the flour into a bowl, make a well in the centre and add the eggs. Whisk, drawing in the flour.

2 Continue whisking, pouring in the milk a little at a time and gradually drawing in all the flour.

3 Whisk until smooth. Let stand for about 30 minutes, so the starch grains absorb liquid and swell.

COOKING PANCAKES

DEPENDING ON PANCAKE SIZE required, use a 16cm or 20–23cm pan: a nonstick omelette pan or pancake pan is ideal. Heat over medium heat for 1–2 minutes, then wipe it with a wad of kitchen paper dipped in sunflower oil.

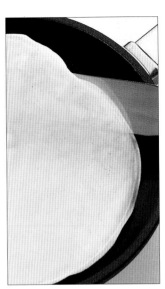

1 Ladle enough batter into the greased hot pan to cover the base, tilting the pan so that it spreads evenly.

2 Cook over medium heat for 60 seconds or until golden underneath. Loosen the edge and flip the pancake over.

3 Cook the other side of the pancake for 30 seconds or until golden. Slide on to a plate. Reheat the pan and oil it again before making the next pancake. A 16cm pan will make twelve pancakes, a 23cm pan will make eight.

RICE & PASTA

It is essential to know how to cook rice and pasta well: they provide

vital carbohydrates, and are the basis for a huge variety of dishes.

The methods shown here are easy to follow – and foolproof.

── COOKING RICE ──

THE ABSORPTION METHOD shown here is best, especially for long-grain and basmati rice, and a measuring jug is the easiest and most accurate way to gauge quantities.

1 For four people, measure 300ml rice in a measuring jug. Pour it into a 2.5-litre pan. Measure 600ml water in the same jug.

2 Add the water to the rice, then add 1 tsp salt and bring to the boil over medium heat. Stir once, then lower the heat to a gentle simmer.

3 Cover the pan tightly and cook gently for the time stated (see right). Keep covered during cooking.

── TESTING & SERVING RICE ──

COOKING TIMES VARY, so check the packet first. As a general rule, cook white long-grain rice 12–15 minutes, brown rice 20–30 minutes, basmati rice 10–15 minutes.

1 At the end of the cooking time, lift the lid and check that the top of the rice is dry. Tilt the pan to see if all the water has been absorbed.

2 Cook for a little longer if there is still some water left. When all the water has gone, the rice will be tender and the grains separate.

3 Remove the pan from the heat. Let stand, covered, for 5 minutes. Before serving, fluff up the rice with a fork.

COOKING PASTA

FOR FOUR PEOPLE, allow 4 litres water, 1 tbsp salt and 400g dried pasta/500g fresh pasta. Most dried shapes cook in 10–15 minutes, fresh in 2–3 minutes, but check the packet and test for doneness just before the recommended time. Shapes like penne, gnocchi and conchiglie trap water, so always drain these thoroughly.

COOKING SPAGHETTI

THIS LONG PASTA is cooked in the same way as any other pasta (see left), but it requires a little extra care at the beginning – even the shorter lengths of spaghetti are unlikely to fit into your pan without softening first. Fresh spaghetti is an exception because it is soft; it cooks very quickly – check the packet for exact time.

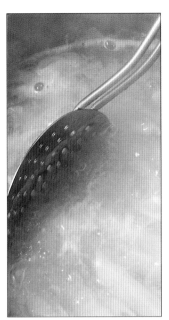
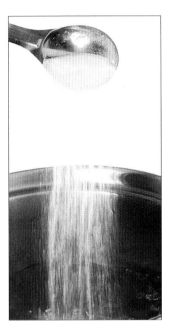

1 Bring the water to the boil in a 5-litre pan. Add the salt, then the pasta, and bring back to the boil. Set a timer for the recommended time.

2 Cook, uncovered, over high heat. Stir often with a slotted spoon during cooking, to prevent the shapes sticking to one another.

1 Bring the water to the boil in a 5-litre pan. Add the salt after the water has started to boil, then lower one end of the spaghetti into the water.

2 As the spaghetti softens, coil it into the water until it is submerged. Start timing from this moment, and stir often to keep the strands separate.

NOODLES

DRIED CHINESE EGG NOODLES come conveniently packed in flat sheets. Three sheets, weighing 250g in total, are enough for four people. Cooking methods differ from one brand to another, but this is one of the quickest and most efficient ways to prepare them.

3 Just before the time is up, lift out some pasta and pinch it with your fingers, or bite into it. It should be tender, but retain some bite (*al dente*).

4 Remove the pan from the heat and drain the pasta in a large colander. Shake the colander vigorously to drain off as much water as possible.

1 Bring plenty of water to the boil in a 5-litre pan. Add the noodles and stir to separate them. Remove the pan from the heat.

2 Cover the pan and let stand for 6 minutes. Drain the noodles thoroughly in a colander. Toss noodles with 1–2 tsp sesame oil, if you like.

GRAINS & PULSES

The combination of grains and pulses is nature's power-pack.

When eaten together they provide a complete source of protein:

low in fat, high in vitamins, minerals and fibre, and tasty too.

BULGAR WHEAT

ALSO KNOWN AS BURGHUL, this is wheat that has been pre-cooked, dried and crushed. It is extremely quick and simple to prepare – it only needs to be soaked before use. For four people you will need about 100g bulgar: serve it warm in pilafs or cold in salads like tabbouleh.

 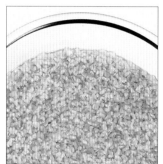

1 Put the bulgar in a large bowl. Add enough cold water to cover it generously. Let stand for 20–30 minutes.

2 Tip the bulgar into a sieve and squeeze it with your hands to remove as much excess water as possible.

COUSCOUS

COUSCOUS IS A PRE-COOKED product made from wheat. The traditional Moroccan cooking method is to steam it in a special pan over a meat or vegetable stew, but a quick alternative is shown here. To serve four, use 400ml water, 1 tsp salt, 1 tbsp olive oil and 250g couscous.

1 Bring the water to the boil in a 2.5-litre pan. Add the salt, oil and couscous. Remove from the heat, stir and cover the pan.

2 Let stand for 5 minutes, return to the hob and cook over medium heat, stirring with a fork, for 3–5 minutes.

POLENTA

LIKE MASHED POTATO, boiled polenta is good with meat, poultry and casseroles with lots of sauce. Instructions are given here for instant polenta, which is easier to cook than ordinary polenta. For four people, allow 1 litre water, 1 tsp salt, 250g polenta and 50g butter.

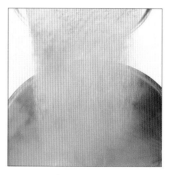 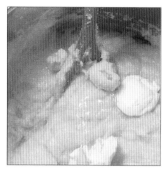

1 Bring the water to the boil in a 5-litre pan. Add the salt, then pour in the polenta in a steady stream.

2 Cook over very low heat, stirring constantly, until it pulls away from the pan, about 8 minutes. Add the butter.

3 Remove from the heat and beat until the polenta holds its shape. Check seasoning.

LENTILS

FOR THE BUSY COOK, lentils are invaluable because, unlike other pulses, they do not need soaking – and they cook in double-quick time. Red and orange lentils cook down to a soft, mushy consistency and are often served as a side dish or in Indian dhal; green, Puy and brown lentils hold their shape and are good in salads. For all types, use 250g lentils and 600ml water to serve four.

DRIED BEANS & PEAS

ALL PULSES EXCEPT LENTILS need soaking overnight, then boiling rapidly for 10 minutes to destroy any toxins. Cooking times range from 45 minutes for aduki beans to 2 hours for chickpeas; most beans take 1–1½ hours. For more precise times, see page 161, and check the packet. Skim off scum during cooking with a slotted spoon. Once cooked, drain and use in salads, purées and stews.

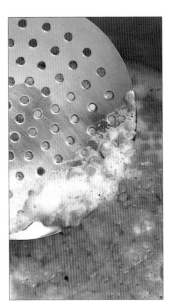

1 Rinse the lentils in a sieve under cold running water, then put them in a pan with the water. Bring to the boil.

2 Skim off the scum with a slotted spoon. Cook, uncovered, over medium heat for 20–30 minutes.

1 Put beans or peas in a large bowl and cover generously with cold water. Let soak for at least 8 hours. Drain and rinse.

2 Put the beans or peas in a pan; cover generously with cold water. Bring to the boil and boil rapidly for 10 minutes.

3 Check that all the water has been absorbed and the lentils are tender. Add salt to taste.

3 Reduce the heat to low, cover and simmer gently until tender. To test, squeeze gently – they should feel soft through to the centre.

FISH

Fish is nutritious, low in fat and quick to cook. At the supermarket

and fishmonger it is sold ready gutted and scaled, and

often cut into serving portions, so very little preparation is needed.

BUYING

WHEN CHOOSING FISH, look for firm, moist flesh, and ask for it to be cut while you wait. All the fish shown here are easy to find, prepare and cook. A whole fish weighing 350–500g is enough for one person; for fillets, allow 125–175g per person.

Whole trout *for baking, grilling and poaching. Try sea bass and mullet too.*

Sole fillets *for pan-frying and grilling. Treat plaice fillets in the same way.*

Salmon fillets *for char-grilling, grilling, pan-frying and baking. Sea bass fillets can be cooked like this too.*

Cod steak *for pan-frying, grilling, poaching and baking. Salmon steaks can be cooked in the same way.*

Haddock fillet *for grilling, pan-frying and baking. Cook cod and hake fillets the same way.*

PREPARING A WHOLE FISH

THIS IS ONE OF THE BEST WAYS TO PREPARE a whole fish for grilling or baking. The trimming of the fins and tail gives the fish a neat, attractive appearance, and lemon slices and herbs impart flavour to the flesh. For extra moistness, brush skin with olive oil before cooking.

1 Using kitchen scissors, cut all the fins off the back and the stomach of the fish. Discard the fins.

2 Cut the tail into a neat "V" shape. Rinse the fish under cold running water, then pat thoroughly dry.

3 Using a chef's knife, make several diagonal slashes in each side of the fish, cutting right down to the bone.

4 Insert a few sprigs of fresh parsley and a lemon slice in each slash, then sprinkle the fish with salt and pepper.

42

PREPARING FILLETS

INDIVIDUAL FILLETS ARE CONVENIENT because they cook very quickly. Salmon is shown here, but haddock, hake, sea bass and cod can be prepared in the same way. Fish is sometimes sold in a long piece, which is one side of the fish after it has been filleted – this will need to be cut into individual servings of 125–175g. One of the quickest and tastiest ways to cook salmon fillets is by char-grilling – see the Master Recipe on page 92.

1 Run your fingertips along the flesh to feel for tiny pin bones. Pull out with a pair of tweezers or with your fingers.

2 Using a chef's knife, trim any ragged skin or fat from the edges of the fillet so you are left with a neat shape.

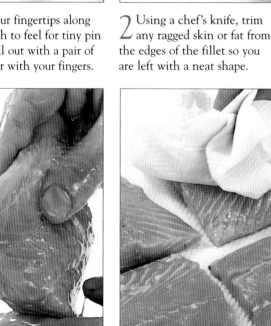

3 Rinse for a few seconds under cold running water, rubbing the skin with your fingers to dislodge any scales.

4 Lay the fillets skin-side down on kitchen paper. Pat them dry with more kitchen paper before cooking.

SKINNING FILLETS

A FISHMONGER WILL REMOVE the skin from fish fillets if asked, but most packaged fish from supermarkets comes with the skin on. It can be cooked like this, and the skin will help hold the flesh together, but you may prefer to remove it. If the fish is to be coated before cooking, the skin must be removed. Fish fillets are slippery, so dip your fingers in salt to get a firm grip on the fish before skinning. Use a chef's knife to cut.

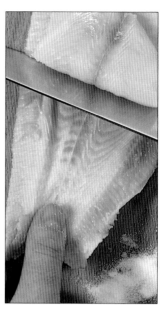

1 Skin-side down, grip the tail end of the fish between salted index finger and thumb.

2 Working away from you with a sawing action, cut between the skin and flesh.

COATING FILLETS

EGG AND BREADCRUMBS make a crunchy coating and protect fish during cooking. For 4 fillets, use 1 large egg and 75g fresh or dried breadcrumbs (see page 70). Make sure the fish is absolutely dry, and sprinkle the crumbs on a sheet of greaseproof paper before you start.

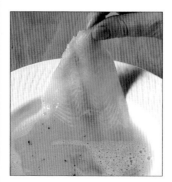 

1 Beat the egg in a shallow dish. Dip the fillet in the egg, turn it to coat, then lift it up to drain off the excess egg.

2 Transfer the fillet to the breadcrumbs. Lift the sides of the paper and shake the crumbs over the fish to coat.

SHELLFISH

A good source of low-fat protein, fresh and frozen shellfish are now

available in most supermarkets. If you follow the simple techniques

shown here, you will find they are easy to prepare and cook.

BUYING

GENERALLY SPEAKING, IT IS BEST to buy raw shellfish and cook it yourself. It will taste fresher, and have juicier flesh than shellfish that is bought ready-cooked. Fresh mussels and clams are generally sold raw and alive in their shells; if they are shelled they are stored in brine.

Scallop *with orange coral in shell. For stir-frying, pan-frying and grilling.*

Tiger prawns *raw (top) and cooked. For grilling, stir-frying and pan-frying.*

Tiger prawns with heads removed *raw (left) and cooked. For stir-frying and pan-frying.*

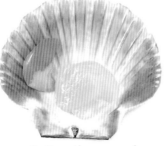

Mussels *small for stews and soups; large for steaming, grilling and baking.*

Small palourde clams *for soups and stews. Venus and amandes are similar.*

Cooked prawns in their shells *for eating cold, and in salads and stir-fries.*

Peeled cooked prawns *for eating cold, and in salads, soups and stir-fries.*

Large quahog clams *for steaming, baking, stuffings and chowders.*

MUSSELS

ANY MUSSELS THAT HAVE BROKEN SHELLS, or open shells that do not close when tapped hard on the work surface, will be dead. Discard them. Always cook mussels on the day of purchase. To cook them, see the recipe on page 127. Buy about 2kg mussels to serve four people.

1 Detach and discard the stringy "beard" from the shell by pulling it away with the help of a paring knife.

2 With the back of the same knife, scrape any barnacles off the mussels, always working away from you.

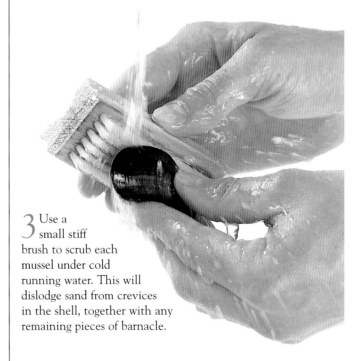

3 Use a small stiff brush to scrub each mussel under cold running water. This will dislodge sand from crevices in the shell, together with any remaining pieces of barnacle.

SCALLOPS

SHELLED SCALLOPS are the most commonly available. They should have a sweet, fresh smell and plump, creamy flesh. Often the orange coral is still attached – this is the roe, which is edible and looks attractive when sliced and cooked with the white meat. Whichever cooking method you choose, all scallops cook in 3–4 minutes, so do not exceed this time or they will be rubbery. Allow 3–4 large scallops, or 10 small "queen" scallops, per person.

 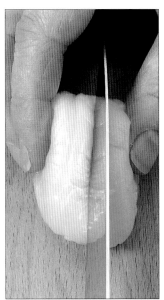

1 Using kitchen scissors, cut off the crescent-shaped muscle on the side of the white body. Discard it because it is tough and chewy.

2 Large scallops cook best if sliced. Using a chef's knife, slice through into rounds. Small queen scallops can be left whole.

CLAMS

AFTER CLEANING, clams should be steamed in a covered pan for about 5 minutes until they are fully open. They are then ready to eat, or may be used in soups and stews. Allow 375–500g small clams or 2–3 quahogs per person.

Live clams in their shells must be cleaned before cooking. Start by soaking them for at least 1 hour in cold salted water (4 tbsp salt to 1 litre water) – this will help dislodge some of the sand. After soaking, drain the clams and scrub them hard with a stiff brush under cold running water to remove any remaining sand and grit (unlike mussels, there is no stringy "beard"). As you work, discard any open clams or clams with broken shells.

PRAWNS

IN THEIR RAW STATE, prawns are grey; it is only when they are cooked that they turn the more familiar pink. Whether raw or cooked, the shell is removed in the same way. The dark vein that runs through a prawn is edible, but unsightly and can be gritty in large prawns. Remove as shown below. Allow 3–4 tiger prawns per person, about 200g prawns in their shells per person, or 125g peeled cooked prawns.

1 If the head is still on the prawn, pinch it between your fingers and pull it from the body to leave just the fleshy tail end intact.

2 Peel the shell from the body with your fingers, working down from the head. When you reach the tail, pull the meat out of the shell.

3 If the prawn is large, remove the dark vein: make a shallow cut along the back of the prawn with a paring knife to reveal it.

4 Pick out the end of the vein with the tip of the knife; gently pull it out, starting from the head end. Discard the vein.

POULTRY

Inexpensive and quick-cooking, poultry requires very little in the way of preparation and marries well with other flavours. Most is low in fat and even the newest cook can achieve consistently good results.

BIRDS FOR ROASTING

THERE IS A WIDE CHOICE of birds for roasting. Free-range generally have the best flavour; corn-fed have a good colour, but are not always free-range. Frozen birds are good value, and less expensive than fresh. For defrosting times and roasting temperatures and times, see page 160.

Chicken *should have light, moist skin and a plump breast. 1.5–1.8kg serves 3–4; 2.5–3kg serves 6–8.*

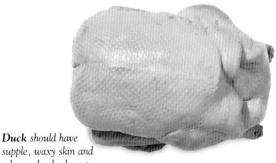

Duck *should have supple, waxy skin and a long, slender breast. 1.8kg serves 2; 2.5kg serves 4.*

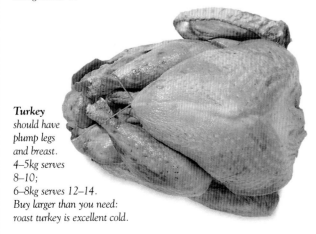

Turkey *should have plump legs and breast. 4–5kg serves 8–10; 6–8kg serves 12–14. Buy larger than you need: roast turkey is excellent cold.*

CUTS OF POULTRY

INDIVIDUAL PIECES OF POULTRY cook much quicker than whole birds, and make portion control easier. They require little preparation and are extremely versatile. For each person allow 100–175g boneless meat, a little more if meat is on the bone.

Chicken wing with breast *for pan-frying, grilling and casseroles.*

Whole chicken leg *for casseroles, pan-frying, grilling and roasting.*

Boneless chicken breasts *with and without skin. For pan-frying, stir-frying and grilling.*

Chicken livers *for grilling, pan-frying and pâtés. Fresh have a better texture than frozen.*

Turkey escalope (breast steak) *for pan-frying and stir-frying.*

Chicken drumstick *(below left) for grilling and barbecuing.*

Minced turkey *for burgers: low-fat alternative to minced beef or lamb.*

Chicken thighs *(left) with and without skin, for casseroles and barbecuing.*

Preparing a Chicken

A SMALL TO MEDIUM CHICKEN (up to 2kg) can be held together for roasting by following the steps below. Large chickens and turkeys cook better if tied (trussed) with string, especially if there is stuffing in the neck end (see page 48). If there are giblets inside the chicken, remove them before preparing the bird. For instructions on how to roast a chicken, see the Master Recipe on page 100.

1 With your fingers, pull off the excess white fat on both sides of the opening at the tail end of the bird.

2 Wipe the cavity with kitchen paper, then use a fresh piece to wipe the skin. The skin crisps better if dry.

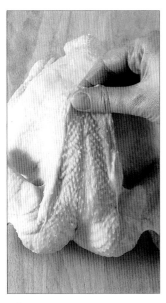

3 Turn the bird breast-side down and pull the neck skin over the neck cavity. If you like, cut off the excess skin with scissors to neaten it.

4 Twist the wings round so the tips come up and over the skin to secure it. Turn the bird breast-side up and tie the legs together with string.

Preparing Chicken Breasts

BONELESS CHICKEN BREASTS have white, low-fat meat that cooks very quickly, but they need to be cooked with care if they are to be succulent and tender. If the skin is left on, the flesh will be more moist, but the fat content will be higher. One solution is to cook the chicken with the skin on, then pull it off with your fingers just before serving.

SEPARATING THE FILLET

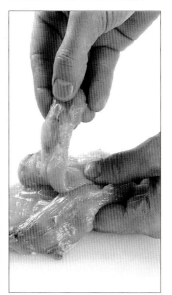

Pull the small strip of tender fillet away from the underside. A choice part, it takes less time to cook than the rest.

MAKING A POCKET

Push your finger between the skin and the flesh to make a pocket. Insert butter, soft cheese, garlic, herbs.

REMOVING THE TENDON

Strip the white tendon away from the underside of the breast using a paring knife. The tendon is sinewy and chewy; discard it.

MOISTENING THE FLESH

To keep skinless breasts moist, score the top on the diagonal with a chef's knife, then marinate or insert herb or garlic butter into the slits.

TECHNIQUES

POULTRY

─ROASTING A LARGE BIRD─

IF THE BIRD IS FROZEN, defrost it thoroughly before stuffing and cooking. If there are giblets inside, remove them. Stuff the neck end only, not the body cavity. A recipe for roast turkey is given on page 144. For defrosting times and roasting temperatures and times, see page 160.

─CARVING A LARGE BIRD─

LEAVE A COOKED BIRD TO REST, wrapped in foil, for about 15 minutes while making the gravy (see page 103). Unwrap, then transfer breast-side up to a board. Remove trussing string and poultry pin. Steady bird with a carving fork. Use the same technique for chicken and turkey.

1 Place the bird, tail-end down, in a bowl. Pull neck skin back and spoon in the stuffing. Pull skin over stuffing and secure with a poultry pin.

2 Twist the wing tips up and over and tie with string. Pull legs in and tie with string. Spread butter over the bird and sprinkle with salt and pepper.

1 Push the wing down with the knife blade and cut through outer layer of breast into the joint. Ease wing from body; cut through the gristle.

2 Cut thin slices from one side of the breast, parallel to the rib cage, to include some stuffing with each slice. Repeat on the other side.

3 Put the bird on a rack in a roasting tin. If you have a meat thermometer, push it into the thickest part of a thigh, away from the bone.

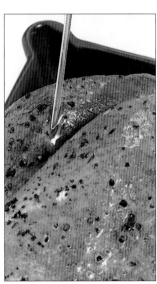

4 Roast until the juices run clear when a skewer is inserted into the thickest part of a thigh. Check temperature if using a thermometer.

3 Remove one leg by twisting it outwards, then cutting through the joint. Hold the leg and carve slices from the thigh. Repeat with the other leg.

4 To remove the meat from the drumsticks, hold the knuckle bone and working from this end, cut thin slices parallel to the bone.

48

ROASTING DUCK

DUCK HAS LESS EDIBLE MEAT than other birds of similar weight because it is fatty and has a large bone structure. Its meat has a rich flavour, so portions are usually smaller than for chicken or turkey. Prepare it in the same way as chicken (see page 47), but remove as much visible fat as possible before you begin. This will help reduce fattiness, as will pricking the breast before roasting and cooking the bird upside down at the beginning. For defrosting times and roasting temperatures and times, see page 160.

1 Prick the breast all over, then rub with salt and pepper. Place, breast-side down, on a rack in a roasting tin. Roast for 25 minutes.

2 Turn breast-side up and roast for 20 minutes. Baste, then pour off excess fat. Finish roasting at a lower oven temperature (see page 160).

SERVING DUCK

A DUCK IS BEST JOINTED rather than carved. To be sure that each person will get a good amount of meat, use the technique shown here for four people. For two, simply cut the duck lengthwise in half.

 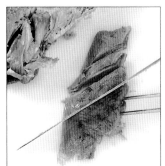

1 Cut away the legs by slicing through the joints with a carving knife. Cut along both sides of the breastbone to free the breast meat.

2 Cut each piece of breast on the diagonal into thick slices. Serve each person some breast meat and either a wing or a leg.

CHICKEN STOCK

KEEP STOCK COVERED in the refrigerator for 3 days, or freeze for 6 months. Makes about 1 litre strained stock.

INGREDIENTS

1 leftover roast chicken carcass

1 medium onion, halved

1 medium celery stick, chopped

1 medium carrot, chopped

1 bouquet garni

1 Break the carcass up to fit into a 5-litre pan. Add the vegetables and bouquet garni. Stir, then add cold water to cover the ingredients well.

2 Bring to the boil over high heat. Skim off any scum, then lower the heat to a gentle simmer. Cover and cook for 2½–3 hours.

3 Ladle the pan contents into a colander set over a large bowl. Allow the stock to strain through.

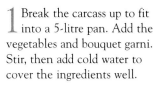

49

MEAT

One of the most important considerations when preparing meat

is to make sure the cut and the cooking method are suitable for one

another. This is the best way to guarantee good results.

JOINTS OF MEAT

PRIME CUTS ARE BEST for roasting, so reserve these for special occasions when economy is not a priority. For roasting temperatures and times of the joints shown here, plus other easy roasting joints, see page 160. For roasting and carving instructions, see pages 52–53.

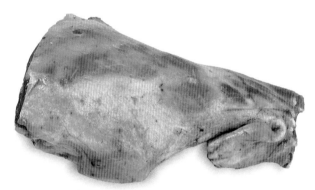

Leg of lamb sold whole or halved, on the bone. 1.5–2.5kg whole leg serves 6–8; 1–1.6kg shank (knuckle) half or fillet end serves 4–6.

Loin of pork boned and rolled, with or without skin. If skin is scored, it will make crisp crackling. 2–2.5kg joint serves 8–10; 1–1.5kg joint serves 4–6.

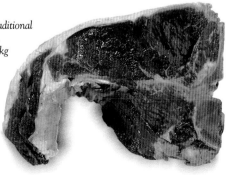

Rib of beef is a traditional joint for roast beef. A 2-rib, 2.25–2.5kg joint serves 4; a 4.5kg joint with 3 ribs serves 6–8. Sirloin is another traditional joint that is excellent for roasting.

CUTS OF MEAT

MEAT THAT IS SOLD READY CUT is both convenient and time-saving. Look for good butchering: steaks and chops should be well-trimmed and uniform in size so they cook in the same time. For each person allow 100–175g boneless meat, a little more if meat is on the bone.

Minced beef sold as fine mince or ground beef (left) is suitable for burgers; medium-ground mince (right) is best for Bolognese sauce.

Chops cook very quickly, and can be grilled or pan-fried. Lamb loin chops (top) have a succulent "eye" of meat; serve 2 per person. Pork loin chops (bottom) are larger; allow 1 per person.

Steak can be char-grilled, grilled or pan-fried. Rump steak (right) is sold in large slices, which need to be cut. Fillet and sirloin are sold as individual steaks.

Pork fillet, also called tenderloin, can be cut into thin slices on the diagonal and pan-fried, or cut into thin strips and stir-fried.

Liver slices can be pan-fried, stir-fried or grilled. Calf's liver (left) is tender, but expensive; lamb's is cheaper. Lamb's kidneys (above) are for pan-frying and grilling on skewers; allow 2 per person.

Braising steak for casseroles and stews requires long, slow cooking. Stewing steak is more muscular, and needs longer cooking.

PREPARING MEAT

MEAT FROM THE BUTCHER or supermarket is usually sold ready-trimmed and cut into serving portions or cubes, but there is often a little extra something you can do at home to make it look, cook and taste better. Most meat is sold lean, but try to keep a thin layer or marbling of fat – no matter what the cooking method, this moistens the meat during cooking and improves flavour.

LAMB CHOPS

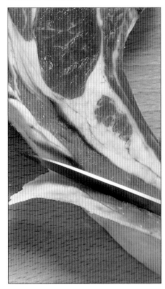

Slice off the excess fat with a chef's knife. Cut around the contours of the chop, leaving about 5mm fat on the meat.

PORK CHOPS

Cut through the edging fat, making deep cuts with a chef's knife. The chops will fan out attractively while cooking.

RUMP STEAK

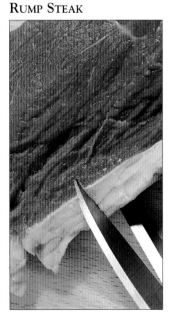

Cut edging fat at 2cm intervals with scissors, snipping through membrane underneath the fat; this prevents steak curling up.

BRAISING STEAK

Trim off fat around edges of the meat with a chef's knife. This is easiest when the meat is still in one piece, before cubing.

TENDER CUTS

TENDER, THIN MEAT is best for pan-fries and stir-fries that are cooked quickly over high heat. Pounding flattens the meat so it cooks quickly and is easy to slice; it also breaks down the fibres and helps tenderize the meat. Here a saucepan is used – the ideal shape for pounding without creating ridges. Rump steak is shown; pork fillet and boneless chicken breast can be prepared in the same way.

BEATING OUT

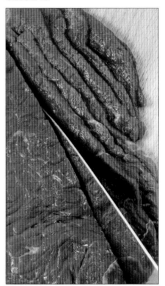

Place the meat between two sheets of greaseproof paper and pound with the bottom of a heavy saucepan.

SLICING

For stir-fries, beat out the meat (see left), then slice across the grain into thin strips, about 5mm wide.

KIDNEYS & LIVER

RICH IN IRON AND PROTEIN, kidneys and liver require little in the way of preparation. Both need careful, fast cooking – a few minutes at the most. Kidneys and liver become tough if overcooked.

KIDNEYS

Peel fine membrane away and slice kidney lengthwise in half. Cut out piece of fat and tubes at core of kidney with a knife.

LIVER

Snip off any unsightly, ragged edges from slices of liver with scissors, then cut out any ducts with a paring knife.

MEAT

— ROASTING A LEG OF LAMB —

REMOVE THE MEAT from the refrigerator and let it stand, covered, at room temperature for about 30 minutes before roasting. If meat is taken straight from the refrigerator, it will be difficult to get an accurate result. For roasting temperatures and times, see page 160.

— CARVING A LEG OF LAMB —

MEAT SHOULD ALWAYS BE LEFT to rest after roasting and before carving. This allows time for the juices to settle which makes the meat easy to carve; it also gives you time to make gravy with the cooking juices (see page 103). Use a carving fork and knife to slice the meat.

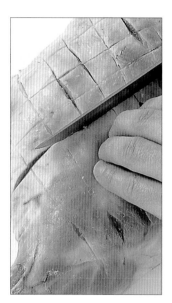

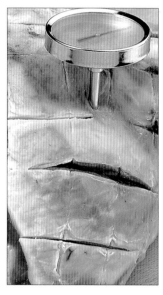

1 Score a diamond pattern in the fat with a chef's knife. If you like, insert slivers of peeled garlic clove or sprigs of fresh rosemary in the cuts.

2 If you have a meat thermometer, push it into the thickest part of the joint, away from the bone. Rub joint with olive oil, salt and pepper.

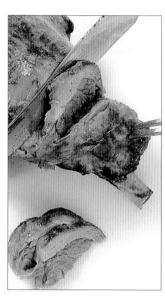

1 Lift the cooked lamb off the rack with two large spoons. Wrap it loosely in foil and leave it to rest in a warm place for about 15 minutes.

2 Place the joint meat-side up and cut a V-shaped wedge at the knuckle end. Cut slices away from this wedge, working towards the fillet end.

3 When all the slices are cut on the meaty side of the joint, turn it over and cut horizontal slices, parallel to the bone.

3 Roast on rack in a roasting tin. Halfway through, baste by spooning over the juices. At the end of roasting, insert knife into a thick part of the meat.

4 The juices that run out will be pink if the meat is medium-rare, clear if it is well-done. Check temperature if using a meat thermometer.

ROASTING A BONED JOINT

BONED JOINTS ARE SOLD rolled and tied, which makes them easy to roast and carve. Good joints for roasting are beef sirloin and topside, and loin, leg and shoulder joints of both lamb and pork. Let the meat come to room temperature before preparing it for roasting. A meat thermometer can be used, but is not essential. Here, pork shoulder is rubbed with olive oil, pepper and salt before roasting to make a spicy crust. For roasting temperatures and times, see page 160.

ROASTING A RIB OF BEEF

THIS IS AN EXCELLENT ROASTING JOINT: the rib bones conduct heat so the meat cooks quickly without drying out. Let the meat come to room temperature before preparing it for roasting. Trim off all but a thin layer of fat, then rub with olive oil, salt and crushed peppercorns. If you have a meat thermometer, insert in a thick part of the meat, away from the bones. Make the gravy (see page 103) while the meat is resting. For roasting temperatures and times, see page 160.

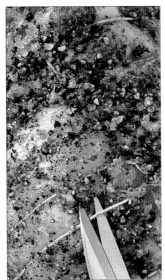

1 Rub the meat with a little olive oil, then with 4 tbsp crushed mixed peppercorns and 2 tbsp coarse sea salt.

2 Roast on a rack in a roasting tin, basting with the juices halfway. When done, snip strings with scissors.

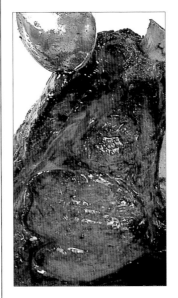

1 Roast the joint in a roasting tin with the ribs facing upwards. Halfway through roasting, baste with the fat.

2 After roasting, juices will be pink if meat is rare, clear if medium or well-done. Wrap in foil; let rest for 15 minutes.

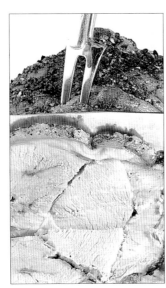

3 Pull off the strings and discard. Wrap the joint loosely in foil and let rest for 15 minutes while making the gravy (see page 103).

4 To carve, steady the joint by piercing it on the top with a carving fork. Carve neat slices with a carving knife, using a sawing action.

3 To carve, first free the meat from the bones. Start at the bone ends and work the knife between the meat and the bones, using a sawing action.

4 Once the meat is free of the bones, position it so that the fat is uppermost. Cut vertical slices with the knife, using a sawing action.

53

VEGETABLES

Buy small quantities of fresh vegetables frequently. Not only will

they taste better if they are as fresh as possible, they will also

be better for you: as vegetables age, their nutrients deteriorate.

ONIONS

THIS IS A SIMPLE TECHNIQUE used by chefs for chopping onions into uniform pieces. Unevenly chopped onions can spoil the look and texture of a dish.

1 Cut off the top end, then peel off the papery outer skin with a paring knife until you reach the root end. Trim the root, but leave it in place.

2 Using a chef's knife, cut the onion lengthwise in half. Put one half, cut-side down, on a board; hold it steady with one hand.

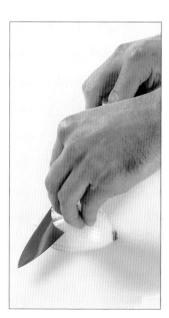

3 Make horizontal cuts through the onion, stopping short of the root. Make vertical cuts down the length of the onion, again avoiding the root.

4 Hold the onion firmly and slice it crosswise into dice. The thinner the slices, the finer the dice. If you like, use the root when making stock.

GARLIC

A HEAD OF GARLIC is made up of many cloves. Prise the cloves apart with your fingers before peeling and crushing them as shown. Purple-skinned garlic is best.

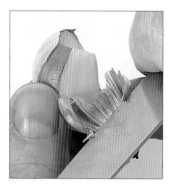

1 To peel a clove, lightly crush it with the flat side of a chef's knife to loosen the skin. Peel the skin from the clove with a paring knife.

2 Put the clove in the grille of a garlic press and squeeze the handles together. The flesh will be forced out through the holes in the grille.

LEEKS

SOIL IS OFTEN TRAPPED between the leaves of leeks, but it is rarely visible. If leek halves are required for a dish, the method shown here is the best way to clean them. If leeks are to be sliced, cut them in half, slice, then wash.

1 Cut off the tough top and root end; use in stock. The tops of small young leeks are more tender, and can be included with the white part.

2 Cut the leek lengthwise in half, then hold each half under cold running water and rinse thoroughly until there is no soil left between the leaves.

PEPPERS

SWEET PEPPERS COME IN MANY COLOURS: red and green are the most common, red being a riper version of green, but yellow, orange and even purple varieties are also available. All have a similar taste, but green peppers are the least sweet because they are the least ripe. Core peppers whole for stuffing and slicing into rings; halve before coring for slicing or chopping.

CORING WHOLE

Cut deep around the stalk with a paring knife. Hold the stalk and twist the core, using the knife to help pull out the core and seeds together. Discard.

HALVING & CORING

Cut the pepper lengthwise in half, then cut out the stalk and core with a paring knife. Scrape away the white ribs and seeds from both halves.

TOMATOES

USE CANNED TOMATOES for cooking if you can't get juicy, ripe fresh tomatoes. Pale, hothouse-grown tomatoes are often tasteless with tough skins and seeds that are difficult to remove. When a recipe calls for tomatoes to be skinned and deseeded, first cut out the cores and score a cross in the base of each tomato, then follow the method shown here.

1 Immerse the tomatoes in a pan of boiling water for 8–15 seconds until the skins split. Transfer to a bowl of cold water with a slotted spoon.

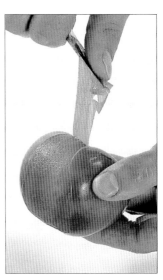

2 Lift the tomatoes out one at a time. Pick up the edges of the skin with a knife, and peel off. To deseed, halve the tomatoes and squeeze.

CHILLIES

THE SMALLER THE CHILLI the hotter it will be. When handling chillies, avoid touching your eyes, and wash your hands, knife and cutting board thoroughly afterwards. For extra protection, wear rubber gloves.

1 Cut the chilli lengthwise in half with a paring knife. Scrape out the seeds and membrane with the tip of the knife and discard.

2 Flatten the chilli with your hand and slice lengthwise into strips. For diced chilli, hold strips together and slice crosswise into equal-size cubes.

CELERY

A TIGHTLY FORMED HEAD OF CELERY with bright green leaves is the best choice. Fresh celery sticks snap easily: if they bend, they are past their best. Remove the tough outer strings from each stick before using.

1 Trim off the leafy tops and separate the sticks by cutting off the root end. Discard any of the outer sticks that are damaged.

2 Working from the root end, make a shallow cut in each stick with a serrated knife and pull down the tough outer strings to remove them.

55

VEGETABLES

AVOCADOS

FOR AVOCADO VINAIGRETTE and filled avocados, prepare as shown here. To use an avocado in a salad, halve and stone, then peel off the skin and slice or dice the flesh. For dips, halve and stone, then scoop out the flesh and mash it. Lemon juice helps prevent discoloration.

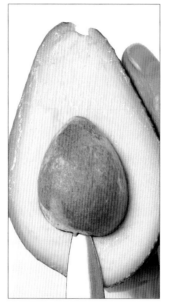

1 Using a chef's knife, cut lengthwise around the avocado through to the stone. Grip both halves and twist in opposite directions to separate.

2 Holding the half with the stone in one hand, embed the tip of a paring knife in the base of the stone and prise it out very carefully.

WINTER SQUASH

TWO OF THE BEST winter squash are acorn squash and pumpkin. Both have tough, inedible skin that is very difficult to cut, so remove it in sections as shown here with acorn squash. The firm flesh must be cooked thoroughly – either baked, boiled or steamed.

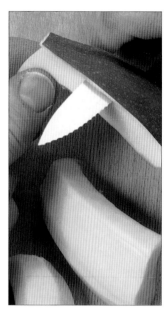

1 Using a chef's knife, cut off the stalk and bottom, then cut the squash crosswise in half. Scoop out seeds with a spoon. Cut each half into sections.

2 Using a paring knife, very carefully peel or carve off the skin from each section, then cut the flesh into pieces according to your recipe.

AUBERGINES

SALTING AUBERGINES before frying draws out bitter juices and firms the flesh so it absorbs less oil, but is unnecessary in dishes with lots of vegetables and liquid, such as ratatouille. Aubergines may be fried, char-grilled or baked.

Peeling is unnecessary. Slice the aubergines crosswise into rounds 1cm thick. Discard the end pieces. Spread the slices out in a single layer in a large dish and sprinkle salt liberally over them. Let stand for about 30 minutes – drops of moisture will appear on the surface of the slices. Put the slices in a colander and rinse off the salty juices under cold running water. Pat the slices dry with kitchen paper before cooking.

COURGETTES

THESE ARE BABY MARROWS. They have soft, edible skin and seeds. The tender flesh has a high water content and cooks quickly. Pan-frying, char-grilling, grilling and baking are all suitable cooking methods.

Trim off both ends with a chef's knife. Baby courgettes can be left whole; small courgettes are usually cut crosswise into rounds of uniform thickness. For large courgettes, cut lengthwise in half, then crosswise in half. If you like, cut these pieces into sticks. Large courgettes can also be cut lengthwise in half, hollowed out and boiled for 2 minutes, then drained, stuffed and baked in the oven.

MUSHROOMS

ALL MUSHROOMS deteriorate quickly, so use them as soon as possible, and prepare them just before cooking. They absorb water easily and can become soggy and waterlogged if washed, so wipe them rather than wash them. Most mushrooms sold in supermarkets and greengrocers are grown in sterile soil, so this is safe. Peeling is unnecessary. To preserve flavour and texture, always cook mushrooms for the shortest possible time.

CULTIVATED

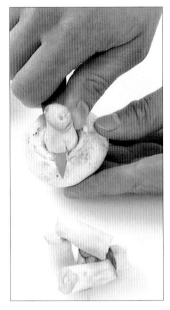 

1 Wipe the mushrooms with a damp cloth to remove any soil. Trim off the stalks with a paring knife.

2 Put each mushroom stalk-side down on a board. Cut downwards into uniform slices with a chef's knife.

WILD

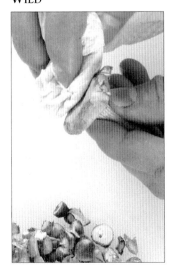 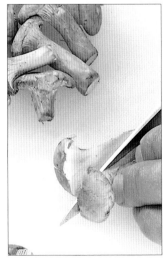

1 Fresh wild mushrooms are delicate. Gently wipe with a damp cloth and trim off woody stalk ends with a paring knife.

2 Cut mushrooms lengthwise in half with a chef's knife to preserve their attractive natural shape.

CARROTS & PARSNIPS

THESE ROOT VEGETABLES share a fibrous texture and a naturally sweet taste. First peel them with a swivel peeler and trim off the ends with a chef's knife, then prepare as shown below. Carrot sticks and slices can be eaten raw; sticks are also good in stir-fries. Parsnips are always served cooked: boiled and mashed or parboiled and roasted like potatoes. For basic cooking instructions and times for carrots and parsnips, see page 161.

CARROTS

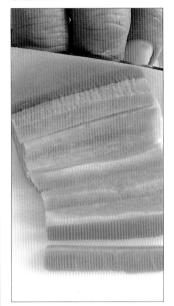 

For sticks, cut lengthwise into thin slices with a chef's knife, then stack the slices and cut lengthwise into sticks.

For slices, cut crosswise into rounds with a chef's knife. For quick and even cooking, make the rounds about 5mm thick.

PARSNIPS

1 Using a chef's knife, cut in half lengthwise, then crosswise. Each parsnip yields two wide and two thin pieces.

2 For old parsnips, stand each piece upright and cut in half, then cut away the triangle of woody core.

VEGETABLES

CABBAGE & BROCCOLI

BRUSSELS SPROUTS are a kind of cabbage. Together with broccoli, they belong to the brassica family and are a good source of nutrients. Eat them raw or lightly cooked. For basic cooking instructions and times, see page 161.

LEAFY CABBAGE

Cut lengthwise into quarters and remove core from the base of each piece. Separate the leaves and remove the thick central rib from each.

HARD CABBAGE

Cut lengthwise into quarters with a chef's knife, then remove the core at the base of each piece. Cut the quarters crosswise into strips.

BROCCOLI (CALABRESE)

Break the florets off the central stalk with your hands. Cut into 2–3 smaller florets with a paring knife, then cut off the stalks and slice them thinly.

BRUSSELS SPROUTS

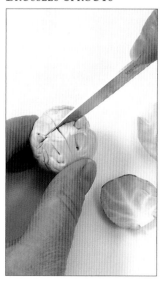

Trim the base stalks. Remove any discoloured outer leaves and discard. To ensure large sprouts cook evenly, cut a cross in the base with a paring knife.

SPINACH

SPINACH WEIGHS VERY LITTLE and looks a large quantity when raw, but it shrinks a lot during cooking. For four people, 600g is the usual amount. Young, tender leaves can be eaten raw in salads; allow only 200g for four.

1 To remove the central ribs, fold each leaf lengthwise along the rib with the rib facing outwards. Tear the rib away from the leaf and discard.

2 Rinse the leaves under cold water, then place in a large pan with only the water that clings to the leaves. Push down tightly and sprinkle with salt.

3 Cover with a tight-fitting lid and cook over medium heat for 3–5 minutes or until tender. Hold the lid and shake the pan often during cooking.

4 Tip contents of pan into a colander. Press hard with a spatula to remove as much water as possible. Return to pan and toss until hot and dry.

GREEN BEANS

FRENCH BEANS ARE EATEN WHOLE or sliced. Runner beans are cut on the diagonal. Broad beans are removed from the pod first, and the pod is discarded before cooking. All fresh green beans should snap easily when bent in half; if not, they have been stored too long or picked old. Boiling is the usual cooking method for all green beans, for the briefest possible cooking time. For basic cooking instructions and times, see page 161.

BROAD BEANS

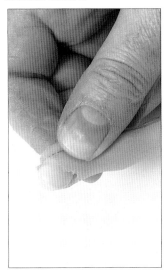

Holding the pod between index finger and thumb, push beans out until the end of the pod is reached. If the beans have visible skin, peel it off.

RUNNER (STICK) BEANS

Top and tail the beans, then cut off the strings from the side with a serrated knife. Slice the beans on the diagonal with a paring knife.

FRENCH BEANS

1 Using your fingers, gently break off the top and tail end of each bean. Leave whole, or cut into short pieces (see right).

2 To cut French beans, line up several beans together in a tight bunch. With a chef's knife, slice diagonally across into equal-size pieces.

PEAS

FRESH PEAS ARE MOST TENDER YOUNG, when they are sweet and crunchy. Mangetouts (also called snow peas) and sugarsnaps are cultivated to be harvested before the peas are fully developed, so they are meant to be eaten whole with the pod. Some very young ones have no strings, and need no preparation at all – these are excellent for stir-frying, whole or sliced. For basic cooking instructions and times, see page 161.

MANGETOUTS & SUGARSNAPS

1 Break off the stalk with your fingers and gently pull down one side to remove the string. Leave whole, or slice on the diagonal (see right).

2 To slice, cut diagonally across into equal-size pieces with a chef's knife. For stir-fries, diamond-shape pieces look most attractive.

SHELLING PEAS

When removing fresh peas from the pod, work over a large bowl. Press the base of the pod to open, then run your thumb under the peas until they are released.

VEGETABLES

PEELING POTATOES

IF THEY ARE to be mashed or roasted, potatoes are usually peeled before cooking. New potatoes should be scrubbed. For safety information, see page 162.

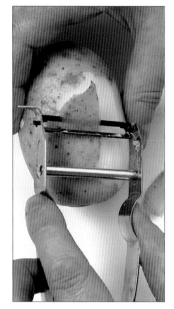 

1 Hold the potato firmly. Using a swivel peeler, drag the blade over the potato in short, sharp strokes to remove a thin layer of skin.

2 Use the triangular piece of metal on the side of the peeler to dig out any indented pieces of skin left by the peeler: these are called "eyes".

BOILING POTATOES

USE JUST ENOUGH WATER to cover the potatoes. Start timing when the water boils after adding the potatoes. Allow about 1kg potatoes and 1 tsp salt for 4–6 people.

1 For even cooking, cut the potatoes into even-size chunks. Put old potatoes in salted cold water, new potatoes in salted boiling water.

2 Cover and simmer gently for 15–20 minutes or until the potatoes feel tender when pierced with the tip of a paring knife. Drain immediately.

MASHED POTATOES

THE BEST POTATOES TO USE for mashing are the floury varieties. To serve 4–6 people, use 1kg potatoes, 1 tsp salt, 200ml hot milk and 50–75g butter.

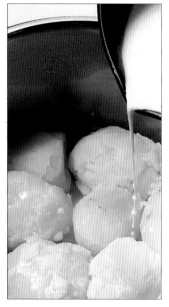 

1 Peel, boil and drain the potatoes (see left); return the potatoes to the pan. Heat the milk in a milk pan until hot, then pour over potatoes.

2 Add the butter or, if you prefer, 2–3 tbsp olive oil. Mash vigorously with a potato masher, or use a hand-held electric mixer.

3 Continue working until all the lumps have gone and the mash is smooth.

MAKING CHIPS

THE SAFEST WAY TO COOK CHIPS is in an electric deep-fat fryer with a thermostatic control. Always read the manufacturer's instructions carefully. The secret is to fry them first at a low temperature to cook the potatoes through, then again at a higher temperature to crisp the outside. Use floury varieties of potato for making chips. For four people, use 750g potatoes.

1 Cut the potatoes into slices 5mm thick, then into sticks 5mm wide. Soak in cold water for 10 minutes, then drain and dry well. Heat oil to 160°C.

2 Place the potatoes in the fryer basket and lower it into the oil. Deep-fry for 5–6 minutes until soft, then lift out and test with a paring knife.

3 Heat the oil to 190°C. Lower the basket back into the oil. Deep-fry for 3–4 minutes until crisp and brown. Drain on kitchen paper.

ROASTING POTATOES

FLOURY POTATOES ARE BEST for roasting. Use about 1kg for 4–6 people. Preheat the oven to 220°C (fan oven 200°C), Gas 7. Peel the potatoes and cut them into even-size pieces. Place in a pan of salted cold water, bring to the boil, then drain – this is called parboiling. Put 3 tbsp sunflower oil in a roasting tin and put in the preheated oven for about 5 minutes until very hot.

1 Lift the tin out of the oven, add the potatoes and turn with a spoon and fork to coat in the hot oil. Return the tin to the oven for 5–10 minutes.

2 Shake the tin gently (this stops the potatoes sticking), then roast for 45 minutes until crisp, turning occasionally. Lift out with a slotted spoon.

BAKING POTATOES

LARGE, FLOURY POTATOES are good for baking in their jackets because they have a light, fluffy texture. When cooked, split and add butter or a filling of your choice.

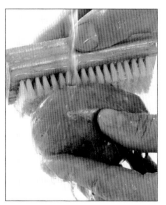 

1 Preheat oven to 220°C (fan oven 200°C), Gas 7. Scrub potatoes under cold running water. Remove any "eyes" (see Peeling on facing page).

2 Prick each potato several times to stop skin bursting. Bake for 1–1¼ hours until soft all the way through. Test by squeezing with your hands.

FRUIT

A wide variety of fresh fruit is now available in supermarkets all year round. High in fibre and vitamins, fruit is essential to a healthy diet. Eat fruit raw or cooked in sweet and savoury dishes.

APPLES & PEARS

TO HELP PREVENT discoloration after peeling or cutting apples and pears, brush exposed surfaces with citrus juice – lemon, lime or orange. Apples and pears quickly go brown on exposure to air.

CORING APPLES WHOLE

1 Hold the fruit steady with one hand and centre the corer over the apple stalk. Push corer firmly down into the base of the apple.

2 Pull the corer up, twisting firmly to remove the core and seeds. Stuff the centre of the apple immediately, before it begins to turn brown.

CORING PEAR HALVES

1 Pull off the stalk. Cut the pear lengthwise in half. Make two diagonal cuts on each side of the base and remove this from both halves.

2 Scoop out the core and seeds using a teaspoon. Run the handle of the spoon along the centre of each pear half to remove stringy fibres.

SLICING APPLES

IF YOU NEED SLICED APPLES for a pie or pancake filling or a fruit salad, the technique shown here is the quickest and easiest way to prepare them. It works well for both dessert and cooking apples.

1 Use a paring knife to cut the apples lengthwise in half and again into quarters. Make a diagonal cut to the centre on each side; remove the cores.

2 Working quickly to prevent the apples from discolouring, peel each apple quarter with a paring knife or vegetable peeler.

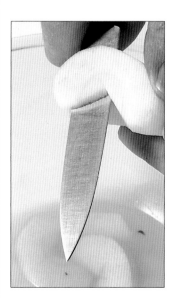

3 Cut each apple quarter lengthwise into even, crescent-shape slices. Cut towards you, following the shape of the crescent.

4 Peeled apple slices will discolour quickly. Toss them in lemon juice to help keep them moist and prevent them from turning brown.

STONE FRUIT

PLUMS, PEACHES, NECTARINES and apricots usually need their stones removed when used in a recipe. The flesh often clings to the stone, especially if the fruit is not very ripe: the stoning technique shown here helps overcome this. Always brush fruit with citrus juice once it has been cut, to help prevent discoloration. The mango has a large, flat stone that is slightly off-centre. It requires a special technique to remove it.

REMOVING THE STONE

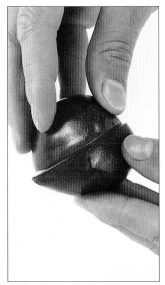 

1 Cut around the fruit with a paring knife, following the seam; cut down to the stone. Hold the fruit and twist each half in opposite directions.

2 Loosen the stone by prising it up with the tip of the knife, then lift it out with your fingers. Thin skin can be left on or peeled off.

PREPARING MANGOES

1 Use a chef's knife to cut the fruit vertically along one side of the flat stone. Repeat on the opposite side to make three pieces of mango.

2 Cut away the flesh from all sides of the piece with the stone in. Remove the skin from all pieces with a paring knife, then slice or chop the flesh.

BERRIES & CURRANTS

PUSH CURRANTS off their stalks with a fork, then wash and dry them as shown below for strawberries. All berries can be prepared in this way except raspberries, which have very delicate, soft flesh and should not be washed because this takes away their flavour. Do not prepare berries and currants more than 2 hours before use. Once prepared, store them in a covered container in the refrigerator because they deteriorate very quickly.

STRAWBERRIES

1 Pull out the green hull from the top of each fruit, using the tip of a paring knife to help if the hull is difficult to remove. Discard the hull.

2 Rinse in a colander under cold running water as briefly as possible. Shake the colander gently so the fruit is not bruised.

3 Line a tray with a double thickness of kitchen paper. Spread the fruit out on the paper and shake the tray gently so the fruit dries on all sides.

FRUIT

—PREPARING CITRUS FRUIT—

SHINY, PLUMP FRUIT with firm, blemish-free skin are best for zest. Thin-skinned fruit will yield the most juice. Buy unwaxed fruit for zesting if possible, or scrub fruit with a brush under cold water and dry well.

ZESTED RIND

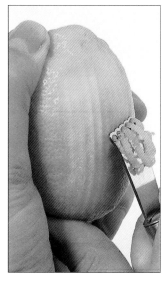 

To use a zester, pull zester towards you, applying pressure firmly. To avoid pith, do not press too deeply into the rind.

To use a box grater, rub the fruit gently over the small cutters. Remove the rind from the grater using a pastry brush.

SQUEEZING JUICE

1 Firmly press halved fruit over a lemon squeezer and twist until all the juice is extracted. If the fruit is warm it will yield more juice.

2 Remove the strainer and discard the pips and pith. If not using immediately, store the juice in a covered container in the refrigerator.

—SEGMENTING CITRUS FRUIT—

TO REMOVE ALL THE BITTER WHITE PITH AND MEMBRANE from an orange, this method of segmenting is favoured by chefs. Always work over a bowl to catch the juice. For round slices, cut crosswise after peeling in step 1.

ORANGE

1 Cut peel from both ends of the fruit with a chef's knife. Stand fruit upright; cut away peel following contour of fruit.

2 Working over a bowl, cut down both sides of each membrane with a paring knife to free segments from the core.

GRAPEFRUIT

1 Cut the fruit crosswise in half. Using a small serrated knife, cut down between the flesh and the inner pith. Work the knife all round the fruit.

2 Starting with the tip of the knife in the centre, cut down both sides of each membrane. This will free the segments for easy eating.

PINEAPPLE

REMOVING PINEAPPLE SKIN requires a sharp chef's knife. The skin is hard and tough, so be careful to grip the knife firmly and to cut with a slow sawing motion. Lay the pineapple down on a chopping board and slice off the top and bottom first so the fruit will stand upright before attempting to cut off the skin. An alternative method for preparing a pineapple is to cut it into crosswise slices after step 1. Lay each slice flat and stamp out the core with a small cutter.

MELON

ALWAYS CHILL MELONS in a plastic bag in the refrigerator before cutting. If not wrapped, they will taint other foods. Cut melons into wedges as shown here and serve them as they are for a first course, or use the slices in fruit salads. Alternatively, peel wedges of melon and cut lengthwise into even slices, then fan them out on a plate. Small melons can be simply cut in half and deseeded as in step 1, then served as they are for a first course, or filled with fruit for a dessert.

1 Stand the fruit upright and cut off the skin. Follow the contours of the fruit removing as many of the spikes and as little of the flesh as possible.

2 Cut the pineapple in half lengthwise, then lay each half flat-side down on the board and cut lengthwise in half again to make quarters.

1 Hold fruit steady with one hand and cut lengthwise in half with a chef's knife. Use a large spoon to remove membrane and seeds.

2 Scrape the centre of the melon halves completely clean with the spoon, then cut lengthwise in half again to make quarters.

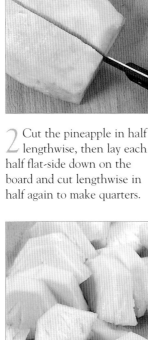

3 Cut away the fibrous core from the centre of each quarter. On young fruit, cores are tender enough to be eaten, otherwise discard them.

4 Slice each quarter crosswise into chunks of preferred thickness. If you like, cut these slices in half to make smaller pieces.

3 Make a cut between the inner edge of the rind and the flesh at one end. Continue cutting to the other end, using a sawing action with the knife.

4 Slice detached melon flesh into pieces of equal thickness. If you like, cut these slices in half to make smaller pieces.

65

SHORTCRUST PASTRY

Making your own pastry is a satisfying task. Once you have

mastered the technique, you will be able to create

an impressive range of quiches, tarts and double-crust pies.

—RUBBING IN FAT—

HAVE YOUR KITCHEN, ingredients and utensils cool, and handle the pastry as little as possible. The quantity here is enough for one 23cm double-crust pie. Use half this quantity for a 20cm pastry case (see facing page). Pastry can also be made very successfully in a food processor.

1 Place 350g plain flour in a large bowl. Cut 175g hard block margarine into cubes and add it to the flour.

2 Using your fingertips, rub the fat and flour together, reaching to the bottom of bowl to incorporate all the flour.

3 Continue rubbing in, occasionally shaking the bowl to bring any large pieces of fat to the surface.

4 When all the fat has been rubbed in, the mixture will look like breadcrumbs. Now add the water (see right).

—ADDING WATER—

USE COLD WATER and add it gradually because you may not need it all. If the dough is too dry it will crack, if too much water is added it will be sticky – in both cases it will be difficult to roll out. Work quickly and lightly, using a round-bladed table knife for mixing.

1 Add about 6 tbsp cold water, 1 tbsp at a time. Mix each one in with a knife before adding the next.

2 Enough water has been added when the mixture just begins to hold together in a soft mass.

3 Using the fingertips of one hand, gently gather the mixture together against the side of the bowl.

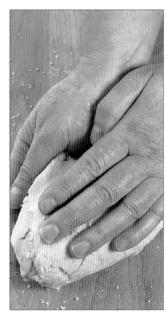

4 Turn the pastry out on to the work surface and very gently shape and pat it into a rough ball.

MAKING A PASTRY CASE

HALF THE AMOUNT OF PASTRY made on the facing page is a generous quantity to make a pastry case in a 20cm loose-bottomed quiche tin. Be careful not to stretch the pastry when you are rolling it out or lining the tin, or the pastry will shrink as it cooks. After you have lined the tin, chill the pastry case in the refrigerator for about 30 minutes, or freeze it for about 15 minutes. This sets the shape before baking and so helps prevent shrinkage.

BAKING PASTRY BLIND

FOR A CRISP BASE to quiches and tarts, the pastry case is often baked without its filling. Lining the case with aluminium foil and filling it with baking beans stops the pastry base from rising up. This technique is called "baking blind". The baking beans can be either the ceramic commercially made variety or dried beans or peas from your storecupboard. Whichever kind you choose, they can be used over and over again.

1 Push the loose base out of the tin. Dredge the ring and base with flour. Put the pastry in the middle of the base.

2 Flatten and roll out the pastry so it overhangs the base by 5cm all round. Fold in the overhanging pastry.

1 Prick the pastry all over the base with a fork. Cut a large square of foil and line the pastry case with it.

2 Fill the foil with baking beans. Bake at 220°C (fan oven 210°C), Gas 7 for about 10 minutes.

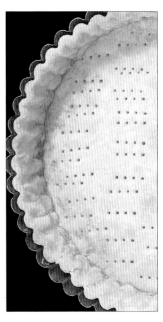

3 Replace the base in the tin with the pastry on it. Fold the extra pastry back over the edge of the tin.

4 Roll the rolling pin over the top of the tin, pressing down firmly. The edges of the tin will trim the pastry neatly.

3 The pastry edges should be a pale biscuit colour; if not, bake for a few minutes more. Lift out the foil and beans.

4 Bake the empty case for 10 minutes more or until the base is a pale biscuit colour. Cool in the tin.

SAUCES

Homemade sauces taste better than any you can buy. These basic sauces are easy to master and invaluable for serving as an accompaniment or for using in recipes. For gravy, see page 103.

WHITE SAUCE

THE CONSISTENCY OF THIS SAUCE is medium-thick. Use 30g each butter and flour for a thin sauce, or 50g each butter and flour for a thick sauce. Makes about 600ml.

INGREDIENTS

40g butter

40g plain flour

600ml hot milk

seasoning

1 Melt the butter in a saucepan over medium heat until foaming. Sprinkle in the flour.

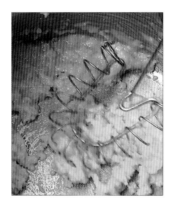

2 Using a coil whisk, whisk the mixture (called a *roux*) for 1–2 minutes. Remove the pan from the heat.

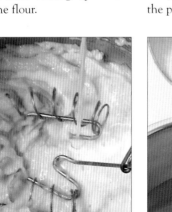

3 Gradually add the hot milk, whisking constantly. Return to medium heat and whisk until boiling and thickened.

4 Check the sauce is smooth, then season according to your recipe with salt, pepper, mustard or nutmeg.

CUSTARD

THIS IS THE WAY to make smooth and creamy real custard, using eggs and a vanilla pod. Makes about 500ml.

INGREDIENTS

400ml milk

1 vanilla pod, split lengthwise

3 large egg yolks

50g caster sugar

2 tsp cornflour

1 Heat the milk over medium heat until hot. Turn off the heat and add the vanilla pod. Cover and infuse 20 minutes.

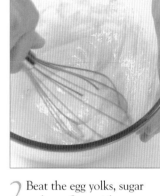

2 Beat the egg yolks, sugar and cornflour with a balloon whisk until combined. Remove the pod from the milk.

3 Whisk the milk into the egg yolk mixture. Return to the pan and stir over low heat with a wooden spoon.

4 Cook for about 5 minutes, stirring constantly, until the custard is smooth and coats the back of the spoon.

MAYONNAISE

THE METHOD BELOW is for making mayonnaise in a food processor, but if you don't have a machine, it can be made by hand. If you make it by hand, use an egg yolk only rather than a whole egg, and make sure all the ingredients are at room temperature. Put the yolk in a bowl with the mustard, wine vinegar and seasoning and add the oil a drop at a time, whisking continuously with a balloon whisk until the mixture begins to thicken. Continue whisking in the oil in a steady stream until the mayonnaise is thick and smooth. Whisk in the lemon juice. For safety information on raw eggs, see page 162.

INGREDIENTS

1 large egg
1 tsp Dijon mustard
1 tbsp white wine vinegar
salt and pepper
300ml sunflower oil
juice of ½ lemon

1 Put the egg, mustard, vinegar and seasoning into a processor with the metal blade; process until blended.

2 With the machine on full speed, gradually add the oil through the feed tube in a steady stream.

3 When the mayonnaise is thick, remove the lid, add the lemon juice and process to combine. Check seasoning. Store in a covered container in the refrigerator for up to 3 days.

FRENCH DRESSING

THIS DRESSING, called *vinaigrette* in French, is a classic salad dressing and is very quick and easy to make. It will keep in the refrigerator for up to 1 month, so it is worth making a large batch. Store it in a screw-top jar and shake to re-mix before using. For a really good flavour, use the best extra-virgin olive oil and a good wine vinegar, and if you prefer extra texture you can use a coarse-grain mustard instead of smooth Dijon. The nicest leafy herbs to use are tarragon, basil and parsley. The quantity of dressing made here is enough for two large green or mixed salads, each serving 4–6 people.

INGREDIENTS

2 tbsp wine vinegar
2 tsp Dijon mustard
1–2 tsp caster sugar
salt and pepper
6 tbsp extra-virgin olive oil
1 tbsp chopped leafy fresh herbs

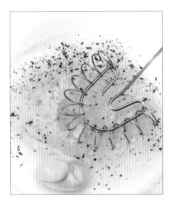 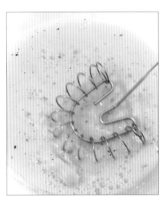

1 Place the vinegar, mustard, 1 tsp sugar and salt and pepper in a bowl. Combine by whisking with a coil whisk.

2 Continue whisking the mixture vigorously until the ingredients are evenly combined and thick.

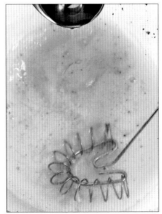 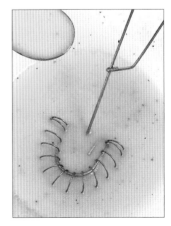

3 Add the olive oil slowly in a thin, steady stream, whisking vigorously until it is all incorporated.

4 Taste the dressing, and add more sugar and salt and pepper if you like. Stir in the herbs just before serving.

CRUMBS & CROÛTONS

Leftover bread should never go to waste – it can be used to make
breadcrumbs for coating delicate foods, stuffings for poultry and
meat, and croûtons to garnish salads and soups.

BREADCRUMBS

FINE CRUMBS FOR COATINGS and stuffings are best made
in a food processor. Use day-old bread because fresh
bread will stick in a ball. Use a box grater to make
coarser crumbs, or push the bread through a sieve.

1 For coating food, pure
white breadcrumbs look
best, so cut off crusts first. For
stuffings, crusts can be left on:
they give colour and texture.

2 Tear 3 slices of bread into
a food processor fitted with
the metal blade. Process until
fine. This will make about
75g breadcrumbs.

DRIED BREADCRUMBS

WHEN BREADCRUMBS ARE DRIED, they give a crisper
coating than fresh crumbs, and this only takes a little
extra time. If you prefer, dry slices of bread in the oven
first, then process into crumbs – the result is the same.

1 Process day-old bread into
fine crumbs (see above),
then tip them into a baking
tray. Spread them out in an
even layer with your hands.

2 Bake at 150°C (fan oven
140°C), Gas 2 for about
20 minutes or until golden,
shaking tray once or twice to
ensure crumbs brown evenly.

CROÛTONS

YOU CAN BUY commercially made croûtons, but the
homemade ones are both easy and economical, and
they taste better. The technique shown here is a clever
way to make croûtons using a very small quantity of oil.

1 Stack 2 slices of day-old
bread and cut off the crusts.
Cut bread lengthwise, then
crosswise into cubes.

2 Place the bread cubes in a
plastic bag with 1–2 tbsp
sunflower oil. Seal the bag and
shake it vigorously.

3 Toss croûtons
in a nonstick
sauté pan over
medium
heat until
golden.

LEAVES & HERBS

All green salad leaves and herbs are delicate and can easily be

bruised, so always prepare them with care, and

store in the refrigerator to keep them garden fresh.

LETTUCE

TO AVOID BRUISING delicate leaves, they should be torn, not cut with a knife, and the larger the pieces, the less chance there is of bruising. To keep lettuce crisp, store it in a plastic bag in the refrigerator for up to 12 hours.

1 Use a small serrated knife to cut around the circular core at the base of the lettuce. Remove the core with the tip of the knife and discard.

2 Insert your thumbs into the hole left by the core and gently pull the lettuce apart into two halves. Separate the leaves from one another.

3 Place the leaves in a colander and wash them under cold running water. Shake the colander and gently move the leaves around.

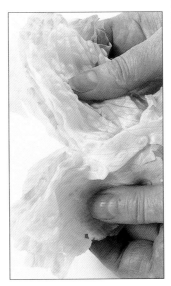

4 Dry the leaves by shaking them in the colander until there is no visible water, then gently tear them into pieces with your fingers.

FRESH HERBS

DELICATE, LEAFY FRESH HERBS are best prepared just before use, to prevent them drying out or discolouring. Add them to cooked dishes just before serving as they lose their flavour if cooked for any length of time.

CHOPPING

For robust herbs, strip the leaves from the stalks. Hold the tip of the chef's knife and chop the leaves by rocking the blade up and down against the board.

SNIPPING

For chives, which have hollow stems, use kitchen scissors to cut. Hold a small bunch over a bowl and snip them finely into the bowl.

SHREDDING BASIL

For soft-leaved basil, prevent bruising by gently rolling leaves together in a cigar shape, then cutting crosswise into strips with a paring knife.

BOUQUET GARNI

To make a bouquet garni, hold together 2–3 sprigs of thyme, 1 bay leaf and 5–6 parsley stalks. Wind a piece of string around herbs and tie securely.

IN THIS CHAPTER you will find twelve
Master Recipes, a collection designed
to provide you with a range of cooking
skills and meals to suit every occasion.
Equipped with these, you will be able to
make a simple supper just for yourself, or
a full-scale lunch or party dish for family
and friends. Each recipe starts with detailed
information on preparation, ingredients
and cooking techniques, plus a close-up
photograph of the finished dish, then
follows with photographs and captions
that guide you through the method every
step of the way. Be methodical and follow
the recipe meticulously. When you have a
little more experience, try the variations
suggested, or experiment with your
own preferred combinations.

MASTER RECIPES

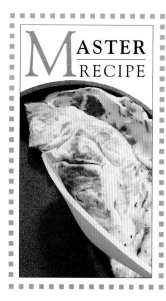

MASTER RECIPE

CLASSIC FRENCH OMELETTE

Nothing could be simpler or quicker to prepare than an omelette: with just a few basic ingredients you can whip up a delicious impromptu meal. The classic French omelette is plain, but the possibilities for flavourings and fillings are endless. Here, the French combination of herbs, known as *fines herbes*, is added.

COOK'S NOTES

Preparation time
3 minutes

Cooking time
No more than 1¼–1½ minutes

Special equipment
16cm nonstick omelette pan
with curved sides

Nutritional information
Calories: 281 (1166 kJ)
Total fat: 23g of which
unsaturated fat: 10g
saturated fat: 10g
Sodium: 327mg

Taste tips
Fines herbes is a mixture of
herbs consisting of equal
quantities of chives, chervil,
parsley and tarragon. The chives
should be snipped and the rest
of the herbs finely chopped.

KEYS TO SUCCESS

■ Use the right size pan. To serve one, use 2 large eggs in a 16cm omelette pan, or 3 eggs in the same pan for a more substantial meal. Too large a pan gives a thin, dry omelette. Too small, and the omelette will be leathery underneath and uncooked on top.

■ Combine the eggs by gentle stirring: do not overbeat. Vigorous beating adds air to the mixture and makes the omelette rubbery.

■ Preheat the pan over high heat until very hot so that the omelette will cook fast, in the French style.

■ An omelette is at its best when freshly made. Once it is out of the pan it quickly goes cold and the texture becomes rubbery: each one should be served and eaten straight after cooking.

INGREDIENTS

SERVES 1

2 large eggs

1 tbsp chopped fresh herbs

1 tbsp water

salt and pepper

walnut-size knob of butter

OMELETTE AUX FINES HERBES is a classic French omelette with herbs, served here with a leafy salad.

TECHNIQUES

Cracking eggs: page 34
Chopping and snipping
herbs: page 71

CLASSIC FRENCH OMELETTE

1 CRACK THE EGGS into a bowl, then add the chopped fresh herbs, water and salt and pepper. Stir gently with a fork, just enough to break up the yolks and whites.

2 HEAT THE OMELETTE PAN over high heat for about 30 seconds, or until very hot. Add the butter: it will quickly start to foam. Tilt the pan so the butter coats the base.

5 CONTINUE FOR ABOUT 1–1¼ minutes until the omelette holds together and there is not enough liquid to flow into the spaces. At this stage it will still be runny on top.

6 TILT THE OMELETTE PAN to one side and use the spatula to fold about one-third of the omelette over. Jiggle the pan gently so that the omelette slides to the edge.

3 AS SOON AS the butter has melted and stopped foaming – the sizzling sound will subside – pour in the egg and herb mixture. Tilt the pan to spread the egg over the base.

4 AFTER ABOUT 10 SECONDS, use a wooden spatula to begin to pull the cooked egg from the edge towards the centre, allowing the liquid egg to flow into the space.

7 BRING A PLATE up to the pan. Tip the pan further so the omelette rolls over and falls on to the plate. The two edges should end up tucked neatly underneath.

VARIATIONS

CHEDDAR CHEESE
Omit the herbs.
Sprinkle the omelette with 30g Cheddar cheese, grated, at the end of step 5.

WATERCRESS
& BLUE CHEESE
Omit the herbs.
Sprinkle 4 tbsp chopped watercress and 30g blue Stilton cheese, grated, on to the omelette at the end of step 5.

HAM & GRUYÈRE
Omit the herbs.
Sprinkle the omelette with 50g cooked ham, chopped into small pieces, and 30g Gruyère cheese, grated, at the end of step 5.

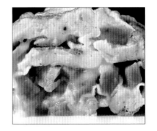

LEEK &
POTATO SOUP

A good homemade soup tastes so much better than a bought one,

and this one is quick and easy to make. It freezes well too, so

it is a good idea to make more than you need. Serve

with chunks of crusty bread for lunch or supper, or swirl

in a little extra cream for an elegant first course.

COOK'S NOTES

Prepare ahead
The soup can be made and kept, covered, in the refrigerator for up to 3 days, or frozen for up to 3 months

Preparation time
10–15 minutes to prepare the vegetables

Cooking time
30 minutes to cook the soup and reheat after puréeing

Special equipment
5-litre pan
Electric hand-held blender

Nutritional information
Calories: 293 (1225kJ)
Total fat: 13g of which
  unsaturated fat: 4g
  saturated fat: 8g
Sodium: 349mg

Serving tips
When leek and potato soup is served chilled, it is known as vichyssoise. For a velvety smooth finish, press the soup through a sieve after puréeing, leave to cool, then cover and chill in the refrigerator for at least 4 hours. Chilling dulls the flavour, so taste the soup before serving and add salt, pepper, nutmeg or cream as necessary. Snipped chives are the classic garnish for vichyssoise.

TECHNIQUES

Leeks: page 54
Onions: page 54
Peeling potatoes: page 60
Chicken stock: page 49
Squeezing lemon juice: page 64
Chopping herbs: page 71

KEYS TO SUCCESS

■ Use homemade stock if you can: it gives depth of flavour. If this is not available, use 2 stock cubes dissolved in 1.2 litres boiling water. Cartons of chilled fresh stock are another good alternative, but expensive. Vegetable stock can be used instead of chicken, and will give the soup a lighter taste.

■ To achieve a really smooth and creamy result, make sure that all the ingredients are soft before you purée the soup. Any pieces of undercooked vegetable will give the finished soup a lumpy texture.

■ When using a hand-held blender, make the soup in the largest pan you have and keep the blades under the level of the soup while puréeing. This will help keep splashes to a minimum.

■ If you do not have an electric hand-held blender, use a food processor or a free-standing blender, but cool the soup slightly first and purée it in batches. If you have none of these, place a sieve over a large bowl. Pour the soup in and press the solids through with the back of a spoon.

INGREDIENTS

3 leeks (about 250g)

1 medium onion

25g butter

500g potatoes

1.2 litres chicken stock

salt and pepper

nutmeg

150ml single cream

1 tsp lemon juice

2 tbsp chopped fresh parsley, to garnish

A BOWL OF GOOD HOMEMADE
SOUP *will do equally well for a
homely lunch or supper, or
for sophisticated entertaining.*

LEEK & POTATO SOUP

1 TRIM THE LEEKS, leaving some green at the top to colour the soup. Cut in half lengthwise, then cut across into 5mm slices. Rinse in a colander in plenty of cold running water.

2 PEEL THE ONION and cut into slices about the same thickness as the leeks. Melt the butter in the 5-litre pan over medium heat until foaming, then add the leeks and onion.

5 AS SOON AS you have added the potatoes, pour in the stock, then add salt and pepper. Do not use too much salt because the stock may already contain some.

6 ADD AROUND 8 gratings of nutmeg, turn up the heat and bring to the boil. Reduce the heat, cover the pan and simmer for about 10 minutes or until the vegetables are soft.

3 STIR TO COAT the vegetables in butter. Cover the pan and cook over medium heat for about 10 minutes or until soft but not brown, lifting the lid occasionally to stir.

4 WHILE THE LEEKS and onion are cooking, peel the potatoes and cut them into 5mm slices. When the leeks and onion are ready, add the potato slices to the pan.

7 REMOVE THE PAN from the heat. Using an electric hand-held blender, with the blades held below the level of the soup, purée the soup for about 3 minutes until smooth.

8 RETURN THE SOUP to medium heat and stir until it boils. Take off the heat, add the cream and lemon juice, then stir and check seasoning. Serve hot, sprinkled with parsley.

81

MASTER RECIPE

TAGLIATELLE BOLOGNESE

Named after the city of Bologna in northern Italy, Bolognese

is a rich, meaty sauce based on beef and *soffritto* – a finely

chopped mixture of celery, onion, carrot and garlic.

Here it is served in the traditional way with tagliatelle,

but it can be served with other pasta such as spaghetti or penne.

COOK'S NOTES

Prepare ahead
The sauce can be made and kept, covered, in the refrigerator for up to 3 days, or frozen for up to 3 months

Preparation time
10 minutes to prepare the vegetables

Cooking time
About 1¼ hours

Special equipment
2.5-litre pan or casserole for making sauce
5-litre pan for boiling pasta
Spaghetti tongs: these are useful for serving long pasta shapes, but not essential

Nutritional information
Calories: 567 (2389kJ)
Total fat: 29g of which
unsaturated fat: 16g
saturated fat: 10g
Sodium: 173mg

Shopping tips
Fresh Parmesan cheese is expensive, but infinitely superior to the cheaper pre-grated varieties. Buy it in chunks and either grate it with a box grater (fine or coarse as you wish) or shave off curls with a vegetable peeler as and when needed.

TECHNIQUES

Celery: page 55
Onions: page 54
Carrots: page 57
Garlic: page 54
Cooking pasta: page 39

KEYS TO SUCCESS

■ Use a deep, heavy pan so the sauce does not thicken too quickly.

■ Cook the soffritto vegetables slowly over low heat. This is essential to release their full flavour.

■ Don't skimp on the cooking time. This is the secret of a good Bolognese.

■ Should there be any surplus fat on the top of the sauce at the end, blot it off with kitchen paper.

INGREDIENTS

SERVES 6

1 small celery stick, *trimmed*

1 medium Spanish onion, *peeled*

1 medium carrot, *peeled*

2 large garlic cloves, *peeled*

2 tbsp olive oil

25g butter

500g minced beef (medium-ground)

1 tbsp plain flour

3 tbsp tomato purée

150ml beef stock

150ml red wine

400g can chopped tomatoes

nutmeg, salt and pepper

500g tagliatelle

fresh Parmesan

BOLOGNESE SAUCE served with tagliatelle and topped with fresh Parmesan cheese is a traditional Italian favourite.

TAGLIATELLE BOLOGNESE

1 PULL OFF AND DISCARD any tough strings from the back of the celery stick. Using a chef's knife, finely chop the celery, onion and carrot. Crush the garlic in a garlic press.

2 POUR THE OIL into the 2.5-litre pan, then add the butter. Put the pan over medium heat and leave it until the butter melts and foams. Turn the heat down to low.

5 ADD THE TOMATO PURÉE, beef stock, red wine and tomatoes. Using a nutmeg grater held over the pan, add about 8 gratings of fresh nutmeg. Add salt and pepper.

6 BRING TO THE BOIL, stirring constantly, then reduce the heat to very low so that the mixture is just simmering. Partially cover the pan, making sure steam can still escape.

3 ADD THE CELERY, onion, carrot and garlic to the oil and butter and cook over low heat, stirring constantly, for about 5 minutes or until softened but not browned.

4 ADD THE MEAT to the softened vegetables, break it up with a wooden spoon, then cook until it loses its redness, stirring frequently. Sprinkle in the flour and stir in well.

7 COOK THE SAUCE for about 1 hour, stirring every 15 minutes or so to check that the mixture is not sticking to the bottom of the pan. If it is, add a little water and stir well.

8 WHEN READY, the sauce will be thick and glossy. Taste to check seasoning. Keep the sauce warm and cook the pasta (see page 39). Pour the sauce over the pasta and mix.

Master Recipe

PAN-FRIED CHOPS WITH ONION GRAVY

Packed with protein, pan-fried lamb chops make a perfect meal

for two for an evening at home, and the flavoursome gravy

is quick and easy to make from the meat's own juices.

To enjoy the flavour of the lamb chops at their best,

serve them as soon as the sauce is cooked.

COOK'S NOTES

Preparation time
5 minutes to prepare the chops and grate the onion

Cooking time
About 6 minutes

Special equipment
Deep 20cm nonstick sauté pan

Nutritional information
Calories: 646 (2669kJ)
Total fat: 76g of which
   unsaturated fat: 34g
   saturated fat: 38g
Sodium: 213mg

Shopping tips
Red-skinned onions are milder and sweeter than the brown-skinned varieties, but if you can't get them, buy the largest brown-skinned onions you can find – look for onions labelled "mild". As a general rule, the larger the onion, the milder it will be.

KEYS TO SUCCESS

■ Use a heavy nonstick pan – the lamb will then cook in its own juices, and no extra fat will be needed.

■ Never add salt before pan-frying meat: it draws out the juices, which gather on the surface of the meat and stop it from browning properly.

■ The cooking time is for slightly pink lamb; if you prefer it well-done, cook for 1–2 minutes longer.

INGREDIENTS

SERVES 2

4 lamb loin chops

salt and pepper

ONION GRAVY

1 small red onion, peeled and grated

100ml red wine

1 tsp Dijon mustard

1 tsp clear honey

PAN-FRIED CHOPS *served with new potatoes, carrots and onion gravy make a nutritious meal.*

TECHNIQUES
Trimming chops: page 51
Onions: page 54

1 TRIM ANY EXCESS FAT from the chops. Heat the empty nonstick sauté pan over high heat for 2 minutes. Grind pepper over both sides of each chop, then place in the hot pan.

2 REDUCE THE HEAT to medium and set a timer for 3 minutes. When the time is up, turn the chops over and reset the timer for 3 more minutes. Lift out the chops.

3 ADD THE GRATED RED ONION to the juices that are left in the pan. Stir over medium heat for about 4 minutes, then add the wine, mustard and honey. Stir well to mix.

4 ALLOW TO BUBBLE GENTLY for 1 minute until reduced to 5–6 tbsp. Add salt and pepper, stir with a wooden spoon, check seasoning and serve with the chops.

STIR-FRIED GINGER CHICKEN

The art of the stir-fry is to cook finely chopped ingredients swiftly in a small amount of hot oil in a wok. Intense heat ensures ingredients cook in the minimum amount of time, so it is one of the fastest and healthiest methods of cooking. This classic Chinese combination of chicken and ginger is wonderfully aromatic.

COOK'S NOTES

Prepare ahead
The vegetables can be prepared and kept, covered, in the refrigerator for up to 3 hours

Preparation time
About 15 minutes

Cooking time
4–6 minutes

Special equipment
Large wok
Wok shovel or spatula (two shovels or spatulas make it easier to lift and toss the ingredients thoroughly)

Nutritional information
Calories: 545 (2289kJ)
Total fat: 21g of which
  unsaturated fat: 15g
  saturated fat: 4g
Sodium: 1074mg

Shopping tips
Fresh root ginger is pungent, almost lemony-tasting, with a knobbly shape and thin, pale-brown skin. You can buy it in varying lengths, simply break off the amount you need. To use, first peel with a vegetable peeler or small knife, then slice into matchsticks or grate on the coarse side of a box grater.

TECHNIQUES

Soaking noodles: page 39
Carrots: page 57
Peppers: page 55
Beating out and slicing chicken: page 51

KEYS TO SUCCESS

■ Cut the ingredients finely, no more than 5mm thick and 5cm long, so that they cook quickly and evenly. Beat the chicken out and slice it into strips across the grain, to break up the fibres.

■ Prepare all the ingredients and assemble them before starting to cook. Once stir-frying starts, the ingredients cook so quickly there is no time for chopping and slicing.

■ If you do not have a wok and a shovel, use a large, deep, nonstick sauté pan instead, and toss the ingredients with a wooden spatula to avoid scratching.

■ The wok should never be more than one-third full. The food should have room to touch the hot sides of the wok.

INGREDIENTS

250g dried Chinese egg noodles

3 tbsp sunflower oil

6 spring onions, sliced on the diagonal into short lengths

2.5cm piece of fresh root ginger, peeled and cut into matchsticks

4 medium carrots, cut into sticks

2 medium peppers (1 red, 1 yellow), cored, deseeded and cut into sticks

350g skinless boneless chicken breast, beaten out and sliced into strips

2 tbsp dry sherry

4 tbsp dark soy sauce

a few fresh coriander leaves, to garnish

THIS COLOURFUL STIR-FRY makes a quick and easy one-dish meal.

STIR-FRIED GINGER CHICKEN

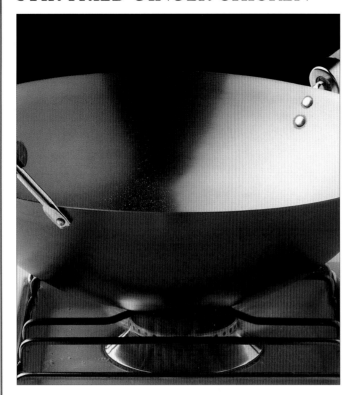

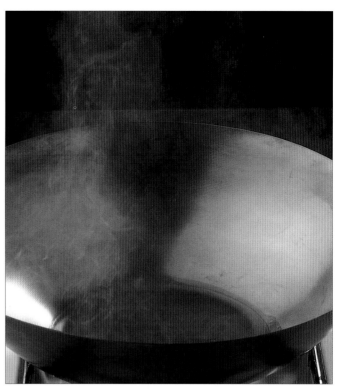

1 FIRST SOAK THE NOODLES (see page 39). Place the wok over high heat for 1–2 minutes until very hot. To test the temperature, add a drop of the oil – it will sizzle when the wok is ready.

2 ADD THE REMAINING OIL to the hot wok and swirl the pan to coat the sides. Heat the oil until it just begins to smoke – this happens very quickly, so watch it carefully.

5 PUSH THE VEGETABLES aside and add the chicken a little at a time. Sizzle the chicken briefly on each side before tossing with the other ingredients for a further 1–2 minutes.

6 POUR IN THE SHERRY and allow it to bubble briefly (this burns off the alcohol but maintains flavour). Add the soy sauce and stir to mix with the chicken and vegetables.

3 DROP THE PIECES of spring onion and ginger into the hot oil – they will sizzle. Stir them around vigorously with the shovel for about 1 minute, tossing to coat them in the oil.

4 PUSH THE SPRING ONION and ginger to one side. Add the carrots and peppers and stir-fry in the same way for 1–2 minutes, then stir the spring onion and ginger back in.

VARIATIONS

PRAWN & ASPARAGUS
Omit the carrots, peppers and chicken. Add 200g asparagus, tough ends removed and sliced, in step 4. Add 400g peeled cooked prawns in step 7 and just heat through.

BEEF & MANGETOUTS
Omit the chicken and noodles. Add 350g rump steak, beaten out and sliced, in step 5; cook as chicken. Add 100g mangetouts before the sherry and soy sauce in step 6.

ORIENTAL FISH
Omit the carrots, yellow pepper, chicken, noodles. Use 2 red peppers, sliced, in step 4. Add 350g skinned cod fillet, cut into chunks, with 250g Chinese lettuce, shredded, in step 5.

7 DRAIN THE NOODLES (see page 39), add to the wok and toss to mix. Taste and add more soy sauce if you like. Serve immediately, sprinkled with coriander leaves.

MASTER
RECIPE

CHAR-GRILLED SALMON FILLETS

Char-grilling on the hob in a ridged, cast-iron pan is a

quick, fun way to cook. Food cooked this way is succulent,

full of natural flavour and low in fat, and with its attractive charred

pattern of stripes, it has the added bonus of looking good.

In order to achieve perfect results, accurate timing is essential.

COOK'S NOTES

Preparation time
5 minutes

Cooking time
About 6 minutes

Special equipment
Ridged cast-iron char-grill pan for use on the hob: most pans are only big enough for two generous portions, and it is best not to char-grill more than this or the pan will be overcrowded and the food will not cook properly.
If you do not have this type of pan, you can cook the salmon fillets for the same length of time in a sauté pan or under the grill.

Nutritional information
Calories: 342 (1419 kJ)
Total fat: 26g of which
unsaturated fat: 19g
saturated fat: 5g
Sodium: 61mg

Serving tips
Lemon wedges make a good accompaniment to salmon fillets

KEYS TO SUCCESS

■ Preheat the pan dry before starting to cook. If oil is added when the pan is empty, it will burn and smoke. To test if the pan is hot enough, sprinkle water over it from your fingertips. It should dance, then quickly disappear.

■ Keep the food in one place during cooking. This will ensure that the ridges leave their characteristic charred pattern on the food.

■ The cooking time given here is for thick pieces of salmon: if you can only buy long, thin salmon fillets, cook for about 2 minutes on each side.

■ After cooking, leave the pan to cool slightly before soaking it in hot soapy water. If a cast-iron pan is plunged into cold water when it is red-hot, it might crack. You will need a stiff brush to clean between the ridges.

INGREDIENTS

SERVES 2

2 thick pieces of salmon fillet, skin on, 125–175g each

2–3 tbsp sunflower oil

salt and pepper

CHAR-GRILLED SALMON served with boiled new potatoes and mangetouts is a healthy main-course dish.

TECHNIQUES
Preparing salmon: page 43

1 REMOVE ANY TINY PIN BONES from the salmon, trim, rinse and pat dry (see page 43). Preheat the empty char-grill pan over high heat for about 10 minutes.

2 WHILE THE PAN is heating on the hob, brush both sides of the salmon fillets with sunflower oil, then sprinkle them liberally with salt and pepper.

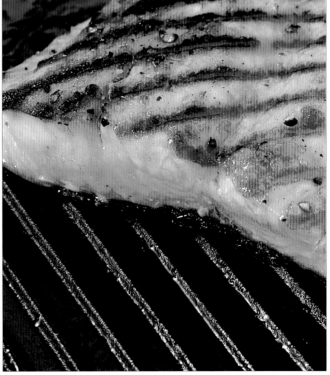

3 REDUCE THE HEAT to medium. Place the salmon, skin-side up, on the hot pan and set a timer for 3 minutes. When the time is up, carefully turn the fish over using a fish slice.

4 RESET THE TIMER for 3 more minutes and continue cooking. Check to see whether the fish is opaque all along the cut edges. If not, cook for a few seconds longer.

93

GRILLED VEGETABLE KEBABS

Grilling browns food quickly on the outside while concentrating and sealing the juices in the centre. This gives grilled food its distinctive charred look and taste. Marinating adds extra flavour and moisture, which is particularly important when cooking quickly by dry heat.

COOK'S NOTES

Preparation time
5 minutes for the marinade
15 minutes for the vegetables
1–4 hours to marinate

Cooking time
8–10 minutes

Special equipment
Eight skewers. Metal, flat-bladed skewers are best, but if you only have wooden ones, soak them in warm water for about 30 minutes before use to stop them charring under the grill.

Nutritional information
Calories: 403 (1675kJ)
Total fat: 27g of which
unsaturated fat: 15g
saturated fat: 10g
Sodium: 456mg

Shopping tips
Halloumi is a semi-hard Greek cheese. Its slightly rubbery texture is ideal for grilling as it holds its shape well. Mildly salty, it should be rinsed with water before use.
If you use mozzarella, choose the Danish sort that is sold in blocks. The round Italian kind is too soft to stay on the skewers during grilling.

KEYS TO SUCCESS

■ Make sure the vegetables and cheese are cut into even-size chunks so they will all cook at the same rate.

■ Lining the grill pan with foil before you begin will make it easier to clean. Always preheat the grill for 5 minutes.

INGREDIENTS

2 large peppers (1 red, 1 green)

1 large Spanish onion

2 medium courgettes

16 large closed cup mushrooms

8 baby sweetcorn

250g halloumi or mozzarella cheese

6 tbsp olive oil

1 tbsp wine vinegar

3 tbsp chopped mixed fresh herbs

2 large garlic cloves, peeled and finely chopped or crushed

salt and pepper

TECHNIQUES

Peppers: page 55
Onions: page 54
Courgettes: page 56
Mushrooms: page 57
Chopping herbs: page 71
Garlic: page 54

VEGETABLE KEBABS
served with couscous make a light and colourful vegetarian main dish.

1 CORE THE PEPPERS, peel the onion, trim the courgettes (see pages 54–56). Chop them into 2.5cm chunks. Leave the mushrooms and sweetcorn whole. Cut the cheese into chunks.

2 MIX THE OLIVE OIL, vinegar, herbs and garlic in a large bowl. Add the vegetables, cheese and salt and pepper, then stir to coat in the marinade. Cover and chill for 1–4 hours.

3 LIFT THE VEGETABLES and cheese out of the marinade. Thread them on to eight skewers, mixing the cheese and vegetables evenly. Preheat the grill for 5 minutes on high.

4 REDUCE THE HEAT to medium-high, brush the grill rack with oil and arrange the skewers on top. Grill, about 10cm from the heat, for 8–10 minutes, turning twice.

CHILLI CON CARNE

There are many different chilli recipes: this is a good basic one that combines both fresh chillies and chilli powder for a unique taste. Be cautious when adding any kind of chilli or powder as it is always difficult to estimate the heat. If you think the sauce needs spicing up at the end of cooking, add a few drops of Tabasco.

COOK'S NOTES

Prepare ahead
Chilli con carne benefits from being made ahead – the cooling and reheating process improves its flavour. After cooling, keep covered in the refrigerator for up to 3 days. It can also be frozen for up to 3 months.

Preparation time
Overnight soaking for dried beans
20 minutes to prepare the remaining ingredients

Cooking time
About 1¼ hours for dried beans
About 2½ hours for the main dish

Special equipment
2.5-litre pan

Nutritional information
Calories: 577 (2424kJ)
Total fat: 23g of which
unsaturated fat: 14g
saturated fat: 7g
Sodium: 628mg

Serving tips
For extra variety, serve with bowls of grated Cheddar cheese, sour cream, chopped raw onion, chopped fresh coriander, salsa and diced avocado. Tortilla chips or fresh tortillas can also be served as an accompaniment.

KEYS TO SUCCESS

■ For a quicker chilli, use 2 x 400g cans red kidney beans, drained and rinsed, and add with the pepper in step 6.

■ Browning the meat is important. Add the meat a few pieces at a time, leaving some space around each piece. If all of the meat is tipped into the pan at the same time, the temperature will be lowered, leaving insufficient heat to seal the meat.

■ Cook the chilli for a long time at a low oven temperature. This allows the meat to develop a tender, moist texture and a mellow flavour. If the temperature is too high, the meat will be chewy.

INGREDIENTS

225g dried red kidney beans

700g braising steak, cubed

2 tbsp sunflower oil

2 medium onions, peeled and finely chopped

1 garlic clove, peeled and crushed

1–2 fresh chillies, deseeded and thinly sliced

25g plain flour

1 tbsp chilli powder

400g can chopped tomatoes

2 tbsp tomato purée

425ml water

1 beef stock cube, crumbled

1 large red pepper, cored, deseeded, diced

salt and pepper

TECHNIQUES

Dried beans: page 41
Trimming meat: page 51
Onions: page 54
Garlic: page 54
Chillies: page 55
Peppers: page 55

CHILLI CON CARNE *served with plain boiled rice makes a good party dish.*

CHILLI CON CARNE

1 SOAK THE DRIED BEANS. Boil for 10 minutes, then cook for 1½ hours (see page 41) and drain. Rinse in cold running water; set aside. Preheat the oven to 150°C (fan oven 140°C), Gas 2.

2 TRIM THE FAT from the meat. Pour half the oil into the 2.5-litre pan and heat over medium heat until a haze appears. Add one-quarter of the meat, spacing the chunks out.

5 ADD THE FLOUR and chilli powder and stir for 3–4 minutes. Add the beans, tomatoes and meat with its juices, then the tomato purée, water and the stock cube.

6 STIR UNTIL JUST BUBBLING, season, cover and transfer to the oven. Cook for 1½ hours, then add the diced pepper. Re-cover and return to the oven for a further 30 minutes.

3 COOK OVER HIGH HEAT for 2–3 minutes before turning, then keep turning until brown all over. Using a slotted spoon, transfer the cubes to a plate. Repeat with the remaining meat.

4 ADD THE REMAINING OIL to the pan, heat over medium heat for 1 minute, then add the onions, garlic and chillies. Cook for 3 minutes, stirring to loosen the residue from the bottom.

VEGETARIAN CHILLI

1 Use 700g chopped mixed vegetables instead of the beef and 2 x 400g cans red kidney beans. Suitable vegetables to use include broccoli, peppers, aubergines and courgettes.

2 Fry the vegetables with the onions, garlic and chillies in the sunflower oil until soft and lightly browned. Sprinkle in the flour and chilli powder and cook as in step 5 of the main recipe.

3 Drain and rinse the red kidney beans. Add to the pan with the tomatoes, tomato purée, water, a crumbled vegetable stock cube and seasoning. Cook, uncovered, over low heat for 45 minutes.

7 BEFORE SERVING, test a piece of the meat and a few of the beans by biting into them to make sure they are tender. Taste the sauce to check the seasoning.

ROAST CHICKEN WITH HERB BUTTER

This is the simplest of roasts, yet easily one of the most popular.

You can serve the bird on a large platter and carve it at

the table or, if you prefer, carve it in the kitchen and arrange slices

on warmed plates. Serve dishes of vegetables separately,

with a gravy boat of piping hot, real homemade gravy.

COOK'S NOTES

Prepare ahead
The chicken can be prepared and spread with the herb butter in advance. Keep it, covered with foil, in the refrigerator for 8–12 hours. Let it stand at room temperature for about 30 minutes before roasting.

Preparation time
10 minutes for the herb butter
15 minutes to prepare the bird
5 minutes for the gravy

Cooking time
1¼–1½ hours, plus 15 minutes resting time

Tools
Roasting tin with hinged V-shaped rack to cradle the bird. If you have a flat rack, prop the bird first on one side of its breast and roast for 20 minutes, then on the other side for 20 minutes. Roast it breast-side up for the last part of the roasting time.

Nutritional information
Calories: 662 (2743 kJ)
Total fat: 49g of which
unsaturated fat: 26g
saturated fat: 20g
Sodium: 390mg

TECHNIQUES

Preparing chicken: page 47
Chopping and snipping
herbs: page 71
Squeezing lemon juice: page 64
Carving chicken: page 48

KEYS TO SUCCESS

■ Defrost a frozen bird thoroughly before you prepare it, or it will not cook through. Pierce the wrapping, then stand the bird on kitchen paper in a container. Leave in a cold place overnight (in the refrigerator it will take 36 hours) until no ice crystals remain in the cavity.

■ For the skin to be crisp, it must be completely dry before cooking, so wipe it well with kitchen paper. This is especially important if the bird has been frozen because it is often quite wet after defrosting.

■ If the breast skin shows signs of overbrowning during roasting, remove the chicken from the oven, cover it with a "tent" of foil, then return it to the oven.

INGREDIENTS

1.5–1.8kg chicken

*1 medium onion, unpeeled and cut
lengthwise into sections*

4 tbsp dry white wine

HERB BUTTER

85g butter, at room temperature

3 tbsp finely chopped fresh parsley

*1 tbsp finely snipped chives
or finely chopped spring onion*

*1 tsp finely chopped fresh tarragon
or thyme leaves*

1 tsp lemon juice

salt and pepper

ROAST CHICKEN *with simply cooked fresh vegetables and real homemade gravy makes a tasty meal that is always popular.*

ROAST CHICKEN WITH HERB BUTTER

1 FIRST MAKE THE HERB BUTTER: put the butter in a bowl and beat it with a wooden spoon to soften it. Add the chopped herbs, spring onion if using, lemon juice and salt and pepper.

2 STIR THE INGREDIENTS together, then beat them vigorously until they are evenly combined. Preheat the oven to 200°C (fan oven 190°C), Gas 6.

5 TURN THE CHICKEN UPSIDE DOWN and roast for about 20 minutes or until browned, then turn it over so that it is breast-side up and baste it with the buttery cooking juices.

6 RETURN THE CHICKEN to the oven and roast for a further 55–70 minutes, or until the juices run clear when the flesh is pierced with a knife between the body and a leg.

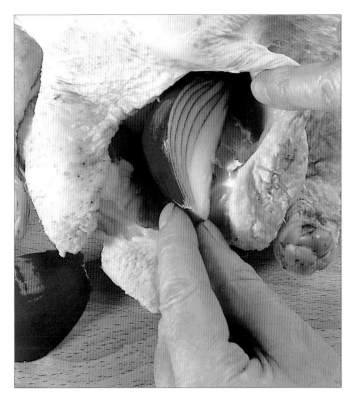

3 PREPARE THE CHICKEN (see page 47), putting two onion sections in the cavity of the bird before tying the legs with string. Put the remaining onion in the roasting tin.

4 PUT THE RACK in the tin and put the bird on the rack. Spread the herb butter liberally all over the bird, then spoon the white wine into the tin.

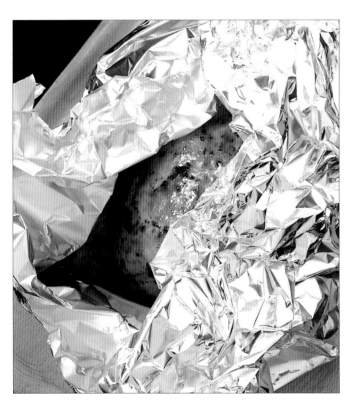

7 WRAP THE CHICKEN in a large sheet of foil, then leave it to rest for about 15 minutes. Remove the rack and onion from the tin and make the gravy (see right).

MAKING GRAVY

1 Tilt the roasting tin so the juices settle in one corner, then spoon off most of the fat, leaving the dark juices in the tin. Discard the surplus fat. Put the roasting tin on the hob, over medium heat.

2 Sprinkle 2 tsp plain flour over the juices in the tin and whisk with a coil whisk over medium heat for 2–3 minutes until the flour browns a little.

3 Pour in 300ml hot stock and bring to the boil, whisking all the time. If you like, add 4 tbsp white or red wine and whisk to mix. Simmer for 2 minutes, then check the seasoning. Makes about 300ml.

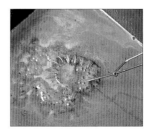

DOUBLE-CRUST APPLE PIE

Homely and traditional, apple pie is the perfect dessert for a special meal. It never fails to please and is easily within the scope of the new cook. The trick is to have crisp, golden pastry on the outside and tender, juicy fruit that holds its shape on the inside.

COOK'S NOTES

Prepare ahead
The pastry dough can be kept, wrapped in clingfilm, for up to 24 hours in the refrigerator

Preparation time
10 minutes to make the pastry
30 minutes to chill the pastry
10 minutes for the filling
15 minutes to assemble the pie

Cooking time
About 45 minutes

Special equipment
23cm pie tin
baking sheet

Nutritional information
Calories: 546 (2292kJ)
Total fat: 25g of which
  unsaturated fat: 13g
  saturated fat: 11g
  Sodium: 241mg

Taste tips
You can use dessert or cooking apples for this pie. McIntosh and Granny Smiths are very good dessert apples for pies; the best cooking apples are Bramleys. Cooking apples tend to turn brown more quickly than dessert apples. Sprinkling the apples with lemon juice as you slice them helps prevent them from browning and adds to the flavour of the pie. Cooking apples are not as sweet as dessert apples, so always offer extra sugar at the table.

TECHNIQUES
Shortcrust pastry: page 66
Slicing apples: page 62
Squeezing lemon juice: page 64

KEYS TO SUCCESS

■ For crisp, light pastry, always work in a cool kitchen, with cool ingredients and tools.

■ When rolling out the pastry dough, take care not to stretch it because this will cause it to shrink during baking.

■ Use only the amount of sugar specified and serve extra at the table if necessary. Sugar draws out the juice from fruit, and if there is too much, it may overflow during baking. Juice that overflows will stick on the bottom of

your oven. Cornflour is added to absorb excess juice.

■ Putting a baking sheet in the oven while it preheats, then standing the pie tin on the sheet to cook, will give crisp pastry and catch dripping juice.

■ Start cooking the pie at a high temperature to brown the pastry, then reduce the heat to finish cooking the filling at a lower temperature.

INGREDIENTS

CUTS INTO 6 SLICES

350g plain flour

175g hard block margarine

about 6 tbsp cold water

1kg apples

juice of 1 small lemon

85g granulated sugar

1½ tbsp cornflour

GLAZE

1 tbsp milk

1 tbsp granulated sugar

SERVED WITH CREAM, custard, or ice-cream, homemade apple pie is the perfect end to any meal.

DOUBLE-CRUST APPLE PIE *Making the pastry and lining the tin*

MAKING THE SHORTCRUST PASTRY

1 Place the flour in a large bowl. Cut the margarine into cubes and add these to the flour.

2 Rub the margarine into the flour with your fingertips until it resembles breadcrumbs.

3 Add the water and mix with a knife until the mixture just begins to hold together.

4 Using one hand, gather the mixture together into a rough ball against the side of the bowl.

1 MAKE THE PASTRY as shown left (for more detailed instructions, see page 66). Wrap the ball of pastry in clingfilm and place in the refrigerator to chill for 30 minutes.

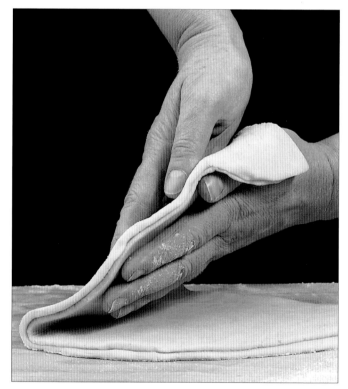

4 BETWEEN EACH ROLLING, turn the pastry a quarter turn and dust the rolling pin with more flour if it starts to become sticky. Do not stretch the pastry or turn it over.

5 WITH FLOURED HANDS, fold the circle of pastry dough in half, then in half again, to resemble a fan shape. This will make it easier to lift into the tin.

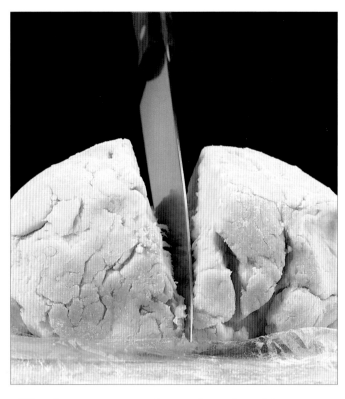

2 LIGHTLY FLOUR the work surface. Unwrap the pastry and cut it in half. Re-wrap one piece to prevent it drying out. Gently shape the other half into a smooth ball.

3 FLOUR YOUR ROLLING pin and flatten the pastry. Working the rolling pin from the centre outwards, roll the pastry out into a circle, about 35cm in diameter.

6 BRUSH THE PIE TIN with melted margarine. Place the pastry fan in the tin with the point in the centre. This ensures the pastry is central and will help minimize stretching.

7 UNFOLD THE PASTRY and ease it into the tin without stretching or pulling it. Do not worry about the pastry hanging over the edge because this will be trimmed later.

DOUBLE-CRUST APPLE PIE *Making the filling and finishing the pie*

1 PLACE A BAKING SHEET in the oven and preheat to 220°C (fan oven 200°C), Gas 7. Quarter, core and peel apples. Slice them, toss in the lemon juice, then in the sugar and cornflour.

2 TURN THE APPLES into the lined tin, then use a fork to distribute the slices, heaping them up towards the centre. Brush the rim of the pastry with a little milk.

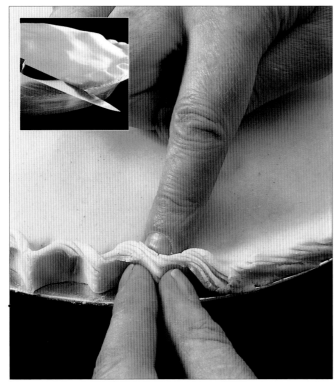

5 EDGE THE PIE by making shallow cuts with the back of a knife (see inset). Flute the edge with your fingertips, then brush the top with milk. Cut a 1cm steam hole in the centre.

6 RE-ROLL THE TRIMMINGS, cut out decorative shapes (see inset) and arrange on top of the pie, leaving the steam hole clear. Brush the shapes with milk and sift sugar over the pie.

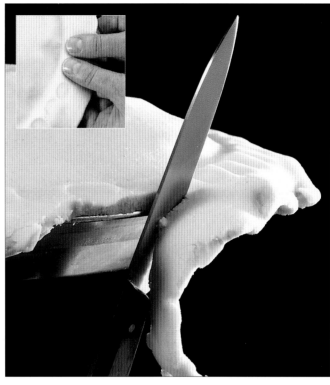

3 UNWRAP AND ROLL OUT the remaining piece of pastry to about the same diameter as the first. Fold into a fan shape as before. Put the point of the fan on the centre of the pie.

4 UNFOLD THE PASTRY over the filling and gently press the edge with your thumb tips. Hold the tin in one hand and cut off the excess, holding the knife at a slight angle.

7 BAKE FOR 15 minutes, then turn the oven down to 180°C (fan oven 170°C), Gas 4 and bake for 30–35 minutes. The pastry should be golden and the filling soft when pierced.

VARIATIONS

RHUBARB & ORANGE
Omit the apples and lemon juice. Trim 1kg rhubarb, pull off the stringy fibres, then chop into 2.5cm lengths. Mix the zested rind of 1 orange with sugar and cornflour in step 1.

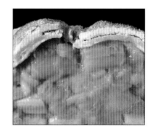

DUTCH APPLE
Use the same amounts of all the ingredients as in the main recipe. Add 1 tsp ground cinnamon to the sugar and cornflour in step 1, and add 85g sultanas with the apples.

PEACH & ALMOND
Omit the apples and lemon juice. Drain 2 x 400g cans peaches in natural juice. Toss with the sugar and cornflour and ½ tsp almond extract at the end of step 1.

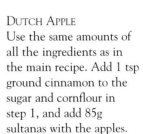

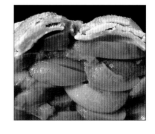

VICTORIA SANDWICH

There are some very good ready-made cakes available, but

once you have made your own you may never

want to buy one again. Not only will a home-baked cake taste

fresher and better than a bought one, it will also fill your

kitchen with an irresistible aroma.

COOK'S NOTES

Prepare ahead
The cake is best made and eaten on the same day, but it will keep fresh if it is kept in an airtight container for 1–2 days. It can also be frozen for up to 3 months: freeze the unfilled layers separately, leaving the base papers on. Wrap each layer in foil and slip into a freezer bag.

Preparation time
10 minutes to line the tins and make the cake mixture
5 minutes to assemble and sprinkle with sugar after baking

Cooking time
20–30 minutes

Special equipment
2 x 18cm loose-bottomed sandwich tins
Electric mixer

Nutritional information
Calories: 511 (2143kJ)
Total fat: 27g of which
unsaturated fat: 17g
saturated fat: 8g
Sodium: 513mg

Shopping tips
If you are in a hurry, you can save time by using ready-cut circles of greaseproof paper or nonstick baking parchment, available from specialist cook shops and the kitchenware sections of department stores. They are also sold by mail order.

TECHNIQUES
Cracking eggs: page 34

KEYS TO SUCCESS

■ When lining the cake tins, remove the base of each tin and draw around each one on greaseproof paper or nonstick baking parchment. Cut out circles from the paper and grease the base and sides of each tin well. The tins must be greased evenly, or the cakes will not rise properly.

■ Soft baking margarine blends easily for this all-in-one method. It must be used straight from the refrigerator. Do not use low-fat spread because its water content is too high and it will spoil the result.

■ Together, the baking powder and self-raising flour give the cake an extra lift, so there is no need for endless beating. Here an electric mixer is used, but you can get a good result with a wooden spoon if the margarine is at room temperature.

■ The baking time is only a guide. Look at the cake after the minimum time. If it is golden but soft in the centre, lay a sheet of foil over it and cook for an extra 5–10 minutes.

INGREDIENTS

CUTS INTO 6 GENEROUS SLICES

175g soft baking margarine

175g caster sugar

175g self-raising flour

1½ tsp baking powder

3 large eggs

FILLING & TOPPING

about 4 tbsp raspberry or strawberry jam

a little caster sugar

FILLED WITH JAM and dusted with sugar, a Victoria sandwich is one of the quickest and easiest cakes you can make.

VICTORIA SANDWICH

1 PREHEAT THE OVEN to 180°C (fan oven 170°C), Gas 4. Cut 2 greaseproof paper circles, grease the sandwich tins with margarine and put the circles inside. Grease the circles.

2 PLACE THE MARGARINE in a large mixing bowl, then add the caster sugar, self-raising flour and baking powder. Crack the eggs one at a time and then add to the bowl.

5 THE CAKES ARE READY when they are risen and pale golden. The tops should spring back when lightly pressed. Cool for about 2 minutes; loosen the edges with a knife.

6 PUSH THE CAKES out of the tins on their bases, invert them and remove the bases. Cool the cakes the right way up on a rack. Soften the jam with a palette knife.

3 USING THE ELECTRIC MIXER on slow speed, beat for 2 minutes or until smooth. The mixture will be soft enough to drop off the beaters when you lift them up.

4 DIVIDE THE MIXTURE equally between the prepared tins and level the surfaces with a palette knife or a spatula. Place in the oven and bake for 20–30 minutes.

7 WHEN THE CAKES are cold, remove the lining papers and invert one cake layer on to a plate. Spread with jam, put the other layer on top and sprinkle with caster sugar.

VARIATIONS

LEMON-CREAM CAKE
Add the zested rind of 1 lemon in step 2. For the filling, whip 150ml whipping cream until thick, then stir in 4 tbsp lemon curd.

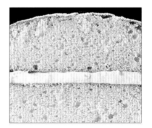

CHOCOLATE CAKE
Mix 2 tbsp cocoa powder with 3 tbsp boiling water. Add to the mixture before beating. For the filling, melt 140g plain chocolate with 150ml double cream. Leave until cool and thick.

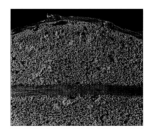

ICED LIME CAKE
Add the zested rind of 2 limes in step 2. Use 4 tbsp lime marmalade for the filling. Mix 100g icing sugar with just enough lime juice to give a creamy texture; spoon over cake.

THREE-SEED CROWN LOAF

Even if you have never made bread before, this simple recipe will enable you to make a loaf to be proud of the first time that you try. It uses fast-action dried yeast, which is much easier for a new cook to deal with than fresh yeast – and a little quicker too.

COOK'S NOTES

Prepare ahead
The dough can be made the day before. After covering the bowl with clingfilm, place it in the refrigerator and leave overnight. Remove it from the refrigerator and leave until it doubles in size, then continue from step 6.

Preparation time
15 minutes to mix and knead
2–2½ hours rising

Cooking time
About 30 minutes

Special equipment
20cm springform or loose-bottomed cake tin

Nutritional information
Calories: 265 (1120kJ)
Total fat: 9g of which
  unsaturated fat: 7g
  saturated fat: 1g
Sodium: 393mg

Taste tips
Strong white flour can be substituted for half the wholemeal flour to give a lighter-textured result. The toppings can be varied according to what you have in your storecupboard. Porridge oats or caraway seeds could be used instead of the seeds suggested here.

KEYS TO SUCCESS

■ Most important is to use special bread flour – it is called strong flour. It has a high gluten content, which makes the dough elastic.

■ Take care that the water is tepid, not too hot or it will kill the yeast. If you mix half boiling and half cold water, it will be the right temperature.

■ Knead the dough thoroughly, either by hand or using a food processor with a dough blade. For a good result the dough should be sticky: if it is too dry your bread will be dry.

■ Bread will rise at any temperature, but the colder the dough the longer it takes. A suitable temperature is 25°C: an airing cupboard or warm kitchen.

■ A hot oven is crucial, so preheat it to the correct temperature: 230°C (fan oven 220°C), Gas 8.

■ Make sure the loaf is fully cooked before cooling. Remove it from its tin and tap it on the bottom: it should sound hollow. If not, place the loaf upside down in the oven for a few minutes longer.

INGREDIENTS

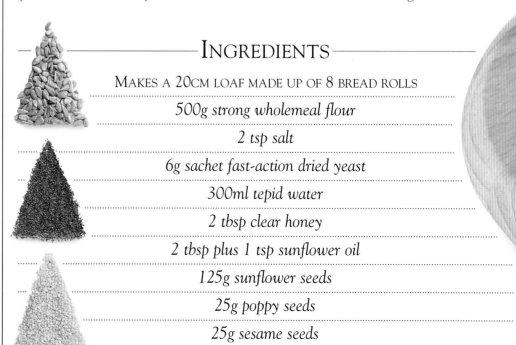

MAKES A 20CM LOAF MADE UP OF 8 BREAD ROLLS

500g strong wholemeal flour

2 tsp salt

6g sachet fast-action dried yeast

300ml tepid water

2 tbsp clear honey

2 tbsp plus 1 tsp sunflower oil

125g sunflower seeds

25g poppy seeds

25g sesame seeds

SEEDED ROLLS look good sliced and served with butter and cheese.

THREE-SEED CROWN LOAF

1 MEASURE THE FLOUR, salt and yeast into a large bowl. Measure the water into a jug, then stir in the honey and 2 tbsp sunflower oil. Pour the liquid into the dry ingredients.

2 MIX TO FORM a soft dough. The dough should be wet enough to cling to the bowl: add more tepid water if necessary. Turn the dough out on to a lightly floured surface.

5 TURN THE DOUGH in the oil, then cover the bowl with clingfilm. Leave the dough in a warm place for about 1½ hours or until it has doubled in size.

6 TURN THE DOUGH OUT and pat flat. Scatter with 100g of the sunflower seeds, then roll up and knead for 20–30 turns. Shape into a round, cut into 8 wedges, then roll into balls.

3 KNEAD THE DOUGH for 10 minutes: use the weight of your body to push down with the heel of your hand into the dough and then stretch it out away from your body.

4 FOLD THE END of the dough back to the top. Give the dough a quarter turn and repeat, building up a smooth, rocking action. Rub the teaspoon of oil round a large bowl.

7 DIP 3 BALLS in poppy seeds, 2 in sesame, 2 in sunflower, 1 in wholemeal flour. Grease the tin. Place the balls inside and leave to rise for 35–40 minutes. Preheat oven (see page 114).

8 BAKE FOR 10 MINUTES. Lower the heat to 200°C (fan oven 190°C), Gas 6 for a further 20 minutes. Release the catch, remove the bread from the tin and test. Cool on a rack.

EVERY COOK needs a collection of tried-and-tested recipes to turn to, and this chapter provides just that. Here you will find a wide range of dishes – everyday soups, eggs and pasta, main-course fish, poultry and meat, vegetarian meals and vegetable side dishes, fruity desserts and favourite puddings, even teatime treats like muffins and brownies. All of the recipes are easy, based on the skills shown in the Master Recipes, so you can be sure of success every time. As you cook more and more of these recipes your confidence will let you experiment with ideas of your own, and you will develop your very own culinary style.

RECIPE REPERTOIRE

EGG DISHES

For suppers and snacks, first courses and light lunches, eggs make

quick, nutritious meals. The recipes in this section

are all straightforward, based on simple cooking techniques.

QUICHE LORRAINE

175g unsmoked streaky bacon rashers, rinds removed, diced

20cm pastry case, baked blind and left in tin (see pages 66–67)

1 medium onion, peeled and chopped

125g Gruyère cheese, grated

2 large eggs

250ml single cream

salt and pepper

*saturated fat 26g • unsaturated fat 25g
sodium 1012mg • calories 742*

1 Preheat the oven to 180°C (fan oven 170°C), Gas 4. Crisp the bacon in a nonstick sauté pan over medium heat for 10 minutes. Transfer to the pastry case with a slotted spoon. Leave juices in pan.

2 Put the onion in the pan and cook over medium heat for 8 minutes or until golden. Add to the quiche; top with the cheese.

3 Mix the eggs, cream and salt and pepper, then pour into the quiche. Bake for 25–30 minutes until golden and set. Serve warm.

SPINACH & MUSHROOM QUICHE

300g fresh young spinach

40g butter

200g button mushrooms, trimmed and sliced

1 large garlic clove, peeled and crushed

2 large eggs

250ml single cream

2 tsp lemon juice

salt and pepper

20cm pastry case, baked blind and left in tin (see pages 66–67)

*saturated fat 22g • unsaturated fat 19g
sodium 433mg • calories 579*

1 Preheat the oven to 180°C (fan oven 170°C), Gas 4. Put the spinach and half the butter in a large nonstick sauté pan. Stir-fry over high heat for a few minutes until the spinach is wilted. Transfer to a bowl and let cool.

2 Melt the remaining butter in the same pan and add the mushrooms and garlic. Stir-fry over medium-high heat for 3–5 minutes or until the moisture has evaporated. Add to the spinach and let cool.

3 Mix the eggs, cream and lemon juice in a large bowl. Add the spinach, mushrooms and salt and pepper, then pour into the pastry case. Bake for 25–30 minutes until golden and set. Serve warm.

CRACKING & SEPARATING EGGS

Always try to break the egg in the middle, so the two halves are even. For more detailed information, see pages 34–36.

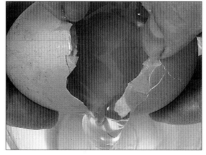

To crack open shell, tap the middle on the rim of a bowl and prise it apart.

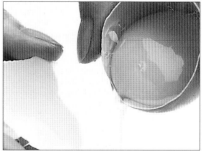

To separate white from yolk, crack egg in half and tilt to pour white out.

CHEESE SOUFFLÉS

If you prefer, you can make 1 large soufflé in a 600ml soufflé dish. Bake for about 30 minutes.

40g butter
40g plain flour
300ml hot milk
150g strong Cheddar cheese, grated
1 tsp Dijon mustard
salt and pepper
4 large eggs, separated

*saturated fat 18g • unsaturated fat 12g
sodium 496mg • calories 409*

1 Preheat the oven to 180°C (fan oven 170°C), Gas 4. Brush the insides of four 150ml ramekins with butter.

2 Melt the butter in a saucepan over medium heat, sprinkle in the flour and whisk for 1–2 minutes. Remove from the heat and gradually add the hot milk, whisking constantly. Return to medium heat and continue whisking until the sauce is boiling and thickened. Remove from the heat, then add the cheese and stir until melted. Add the mustard and salt and pepper.

3 Leave the sauce to cool a little, then beat in the egg yolks. Whisk the egg whites in a large bowl with an electric mixer until stiff. Whisk 2 heaped tbsp whites into the sauce, then gently fold in the remainder.

4 Spoon the mixture into the ramekins. Bake for about 15 minutes or until risen and golden brown. Serve immediately.

CRÊPES SUZETTE

8 x 16cm thin pancakes (see page 37)
FOR THE SAUCE
juice of 2 oranges
125g unsalted butter
60g caster sugar
4 tbsp orange liqueur or brandy

*saturated fat 19g • unsaturated fat 11g
sodium 60mg • calories 489*

1 First make the sauce: put the orange juice, butter and sugar in a large nonstick sauté pan. Stir over medium heat until the butter has melted, then simmer gently for 5 minutes.

2 Reduce the heat to low. Place 1 pancake in the pan and turn it over to coat with sauce on both sides. Fold it in half, then in half again. Move to the side of pan.

3 Add another pancake, coat it with sauce and fold. Move it to overlap the first pancake: repeat with the remaining pancakes.

4 Spoon the liqueur or brandy over the pancakes in the pan and serve immediately.

APPLE-STUFFED PANCAKES

65g unsalted butter
zested rind of 1 lemon
juice of ½ lemon
500g cooking or dessert apples
50g demerara sugar
8 x 23cm thin pancakes (see page 37)

*saturated fat 11g • unsaturated fat 7g
sodium 53mg • calories 336*

1 Melt 25g of the butter in a large nonstick sauté pan over low heat. Add the lemon rind and juice, stir to mix, then remove from the heat.

2 Quarter, core and peel the apples, then slice them thickly into the lemon butter. Toss to coat in the mixture.

3 Return the pan to low heat, cover and cook for 5–10 minutes or until the apples are just tender but still holding their shape. Remove from the heat. Add half the sugar and stir gently.

4 Preheat the oven to 200°C (fan oven 190°C), Gas 6. Divide the apple filling among the pancakes. Fold the edges of each pancake in over the filling to make a square parcel. Arrange the parcels, join-side down, in a buttered baking dish.

5 Melt the remaining butter and brush over the pancakes, then sprinkle over the remaining demerara sugar. Bake, uncovered, for 20 minutes or until piping hot. Serve hot, with vanilla ice-cream or fresh cream.

SPANISH OMELETTE

This thick potato omelette is called *tortilla* in Spanish.

500g medium to large potatoes, peeled

1 large Spanish onion, peeled and roughly chopped

salt and pepper

5 tbsp olive oil

5 large eggs, beaten

saturated fat 5g • unsaturated fat 21g
sodium 113mg • calories 370

1 Using the slicing disc on a food processor, or a chef's knife, cut the potatoes into slices 3–5mm thick. Place the slices in a large bowl and add the onion and salt and pepper. Toss together so they are well mixed.

2 Heat 3 tbsp of the oil in a 23cm nonstick omelette pan. Add the potatoes and onions, spread them out, then cover with a lid or a sheet of foil. Cook over low heat, stirring occasionally, for about 15 minutes or until soft but not browned.

3 Add the remaining oil to the pan and turn up the heat to medium. Pour in the beaten eggs, add salt and pepper and shake to spread the eggs evenly.

4 Cook for about 10 minutes or until the omelette is set on the bottom but still a little runny on top. Meanwhile, preheat the grill to medium-high.

5 Put the pan under the grill and cook for 1–2 minutes or until the top is set and golden brown. Serve hot, warm or cold.

ITALIAN HERB FRITTATA

A *frittata* is a baked omelette. Make sure that your omelette pan fits in the oven and is ovenproof. If necessary, protect the handle with foil.

8 large eggs

150ml single cream

50g Cheddar cheese, grated

25g Parmesan cheese, grated

2 tbsp chopped fresh herbs

salt and pepper

2 tbsp olive oil

saturated fat 13g • unsaturated fat 19g
sodium 339mg • calories 400

1 Preheat the oven to 180°C (fan oven 160°C), Gas 4. Beat the eggs with the cream, cheeses, herbs and salt and pepper.

2 Heat the oil in a 23cm nonstick omelette pan over medium heat until hot. Pour in the egg mixture and shake to spread the ingredients evenly.

3 Transfer to the oven and bake for 20 minutes or until the omelette is just set in the centre.

4 Hold a warmed plate upside-down over the pan and turn the two over together so the omelette inverts on to the plate. Serve hot or warm.

EGG MAYONNAISE WITH HERBS

This is a low-fat version of a classic recipe. The sauce can be prepared up to 3 hours ahead and kept in the refrigerator.

6 large eggs

60–70g rocket leaves

1–2 tbsp French dressing (see page 69)

FOR THE SAUCE

200ml low-fat crème fraîche or low-fat plain yogurt

200ml reduced calorie mayonnaise

1 tbsp lemon juice

½ tsp caster sugar

1 tbsp each finely chopped parsley, mint, basil and tarragon

salt and pepper

saturated fat 5g • unsaturated fat 24g
sodium 643mg • calories 364

1 First make the sauce: mix together all the sauce ingredients, then taste to check the seasoning. Cover and chill.

2 Hard boil, shell and cool the eggs, then drain and dry them. Cut each egg lengthwise in half.

3 Just before serving, arrange the rocket leaves on a serving plate and spoon the French dressing evenly over them.

4 Place the egg halves, cut-side down in a clover-leaf pattern, on top of the rocket. Spoon the sauce over them. Serve 3 egg halves per person.

SCRAMBLED EGGS WITH SPICY PEPPERS

4 tbsp olive oil

1 large Spanish onion, peeled and chopped

3 medium peppers (any colour), cored, deseeded and thinly sliced

2 garlic cloves, peeled and crushed

½ small fresh chilli, deseeded and finely chopped

8 large eggs

salt and pepper

4 medium tomatoes, halved, deseeded and chopped

saturated fat 6g • unsaturated fat 21g
sodium 180mg • calories 376

1 Heat 2 tbsp of the oil in a saucepan. Add the onion and cook over medium heat for about 5 minutes. Add the peppers, garlic and chilli and stir to mix. Cover and cook over low heat for 10 minutes or until all the vegetables are softened.

2 Meanwhile, crack the eggs and place in a large bowl, add salt and pepper and mix well with a fork. Heat the remaining 2 tbsp oil in a 20cm nonstick sauté pan over low heat. Pour in the eggs.

3 Cook for 3 minutes or until very softly scrambled. Stir and scrape all around the bottom of the pan as the egg mixture cooks. Do not overcook – scrambled eggs should be creamy, not set.

4 Add the tomatoes to the spicy pepper mixture, then check the seasoning. Spoon this mixture over the scrambled eggs. Serve immediately.

SOUPS

These soups – some light and smooth, some chunky and

substantial – are all easy to make. They can be

served as a first course, or as a main meal with bread.

PURÉEING SOUPS

Instructions are given in the following three soup recipes for puréeing with an electric hand-held blender. If you don't have one of these, use a food processor or a free-standing blender, but cool the soup slightly first and purée it in batches.

If you have none of these, pour the soup into a sieve set over a bowl and press the solids through with the back of a spoon.

CELERY SOUP WITH BLUE CHEESE CREAM

1 head of celery, trimmed, with leaves reserved

50g butter

1 large onion, peeled and chopped

25g plain flour

1 vegetable stock cube

salt and pepper

425ml milk

FOR THE BLUE CHEESE CREAM

50g Danish blue cheese

150ml half-fat crème fraîche

saturated fat 13g • unsaturated fat 7g
sodium 866mg • calories 253

124

1 Chop celery sticks crosswise into 5mm thick slices. Melt the butter in a large pan, add the celery and onion and stir. Cover and cook over low heat for 15 minutes, stirring occasionally.

2 Dissolve the stock cube in 425ml boiling water. Sprinkle the flour over the vegetables, stir well, then pour in the stock and bring to the boil over high heat, stirring all the time. Add salt and pepper, cover and reduce the heat. Simmer for about 10 minutes or until the celery is very tender.

3 Remove the pan from the heat. Using an electric hand-held blender, with the blades below the level of the soup, purée for about 3 minutes until smooth.

4 Return the soup to medium heat, pour in the milk and mix well. Bring the soup to a simmer, then check the seasoning. Cover the pan and reduce the heat to low while making the blue cheese cream.

5 Put the blue cheese in a small bowl and mash with a fork until smooth. Add the crème fraîche a little at a time and work into the cheese until evenly combined.

6 Stir the soup one more time, then ladle it into warmed bowls. Place a large spoonful of blue cheese cream in the centre of each bowl of soup and swirl it in. Scatter chopped celery leaves on top and serve immediately.

MAKING CROÛTONS

Add texture and crunch to soups by garnishing with homemade croûtons. For more detailed information, see page 70.

Stack slices of bread and cut into cubes.

Shake with 1–2 tbsp oil in a plastic bag.

Toss over medium heat until golden.

WATERCRESS SOUP

50g butter

1 large potato (about 300g), peeled and roughly chopped

1 large onion, peeled and chopped

450ml chicken stock

salt and pepper

200g watercress, chopped

500ml milk

1–2 tbsp lemon juice

4 tbsp single cream, to garnish

saturated fat 12g • unsaturated fat 6g
sodium 303mg • calories 314

1 Melt the butter in a large pan. Add the chopped potato and onion and stir well to mix. Cover and cook over low heat for about 15 minutes, stirring occasionally.

2 Pour in the stock and bring to the boil over high heat. Add salt and pepper, cover and reduce the heat. Simmer for about 10 minutes or until the potatoes are very tender.

3 Remove the pan from the heat and add the watercress. Using an electric hand-held blender, with the blades held below the level of the soup, purée the soup for about 3 minutes until smooth.

4 Return the soup to medium heat, pour in the milk and stir well to mix. Bring the soup just to a simmer.

5 Add a little lemon juice, taste the soup and add more lemon juice if you like. Check the seasoning before serving.

6 Stir the soup one more time, then ladle it into warmed bowls. Spoon 1 tbsp cream in the centre of each bowl of soup and swirl it in. Serve immediately.

VARIATION
SPINACH SOUP

Use the same quantity of young spinach as watercress and remove any tough stalks before chopping. Omit the lemon juice and add a few gratings of nutmeg with the salt and pepper in step 2.

CURRIED CARROT SOUP

3 tbsp sunflower oil

1 medium onion, peeled and chopped

1 tsp Madras (hot) curry powder

10g plain flour

850ml vegetable stock

500g carrots, peeled and sliced

salt and pepper

1–2 tsp lemon juice

FOR THE CORIANDER YOGURT

150g tub plain Greek yogurt

2 tbsp finely chopped fresh coriander leaves

saturated fat 3g • unsaturated fat 12g
sodium 1072mg • calories 226

1 Heat the oil in a large pan. Add the onion and cook over medium heat for about 5 minutes or until softened.

2 Sprinkle the curry powder and flour over the onion, stir well, then pour in the stock and bring to the boil over high heat, stirring all the time.

3 Add the carrots and salt and pepper and bring back to the boil. Reduce the heat, cover and simmer for 15 minutes or until the carrots are very tender.

4 Remove the pan from the heat. Using an electric hand-held blender, with the blades held below the level of the soup, purée the soup for about 3 minutes until smooth.

5 Return the soup to medium heat and bring to a simmer. Add a little lemon juice, taste the soup and add more lemon juice if you like. Check the seasoning.

6 Stir the yogurt and chopped coriander leaves together in a small bowl until well combined.

7 Stir the soup one more time, then ladle it into warmed bowls. Top each serving with a spoonful of coriander yogurt and serve immediately.

VARIATION
CURRIED PARSNIP SOUP

Replace the carrots in the main recipe with the same quantity of parsnips. Prepare the parsnips just before using because they have a tendency to discolour once peeled and cut.

EASY TOMATO SOUP

1 vegetable stock cube

1 medium onion

25g butter

25g plain flour

2 x 400g cans chopped tomatoes

2 tbsp tomato purée

salt and pepper

1 tsp caster sugar

saturated fat 3g • unsaturated fat 2g
sodium 648mg
calories 128

1 Dissolve the stock cube in 425ml boiling water. Peel and chop the onion. Melt the butter in a large pan, add the onion and cook over low heat for 10 minutes or until soft, stirring occasionally.

2 Sprinkle the flour over the onion, stir well, then add the stock, tomatoes, tomato purée and salt and pepper. Bring to the boil over high heat, stirring all the time, then simmer for 2–3 minutes, stirring occasionally.

3 Place a large sieve over a large bowl, pour the soup into the sieve and press the solids through with the back of a spoon. Do not use a blender for this soup: it needs to be sieved to remove any tomato cores and seeds.

4 Pour the soup back into the pan, return to medium heat and bring to a simmer. Add the sugar, then check the seasoning.

VARIATION

TOMATO-PESTO SOUP

Swirl 6–8 tbsp bottled pesto into the soup just before serving. Garnish with basil leaves.

MINESTRONE

2 tbsp olive oil

1 medium onion, peeled and chopped

1 carrot, peeled and chopped

1 celery stick, trimmed and finely chopped

1 leek, thinly sliced

25g plain flour

1.5 litres chicken stock

400g can chopped tomatoes

salt and pepper

50g dried spaghetti

100g French beans, trimmed and cut into 2.5cm lengths

100g green cabbage, shredded

grated Parmesan cheese, to serve

saturated fat 2g • unsaturated fat 7g
sodium 373mg • calories 243

1 Heat the oil in a large pan. Add the onion, carrot, celery and leek and cook over low heat for 5 minutes, stirring often, until the vegetables are softened.

2 Sprinkle in the flour and stir to mix. Add the stock, tomatoes and salt and pepper and bring to the boil over high heat, stirring constantly. Partially cover, reduce the heat and simmer for 20 minutes.

3 Break the spaghetti up into short lengths and drop them into the pan. Add the beans and cabbage, stir well and cook for 10 minutes or until the vegetables and pasta are tender. Check the seasoning before serving, then sprinkle the soup with grated Parmesan cheese.

CLAM CHOWDER

75g smoked streaky bacon rashers, rinds removed, chopped

1 medium onion, peeled and chopped

20g butter

20g plain flour

400ml hot milk

300g potatoes, peeled and cut into cubes

salt and pepper

150ml single cream

100g sweetcorn kernels, defrosted if frozen

290g can baby clams in brine, drained

saturated fat 12g • unsaturated fat 9g
sodium 785mg • calories 374

1 Heat a large pan over low heat for 30 seconds, add the bacon and onion and cook for 5 minutes, stirring. Add the butter, stir until melted, then sprinkle in the flour and stir to mix.

2 Remove the pan from the heat and gradually stir in the hot milk. Return the pan to low heat and stir until the mixture thickens and bubbles.

3 Add the potatoes and salt and pepper and cook for 10–15 minutes or until tender. Add the cream and sweetcorn and bring back to a simmer.

4 Drain the clams into a sieve. Add the clams to the soup and heat through gently. Do not allow the soup to boil as this will toughen the clams. Check the seasoning before serving.

MOULES MARINIÈRE

Serve with forks to remove the mussels from their shells, and soup spoons for drinking the liquid.

2 tbsp olive oil

6 spring onions, trimmed and finely chopped

4 celery sticks, trimmed and finely chopped

2 garlic cloves, peeled and crushed

300ml dry white wine

1 bouquet garni

2kg live mussels, scrubbed (see page 44)

salt and pepper

300ml fish stock or water

a generous knob of butter

4 tbsp chopped fresh parsley

saturated fat 6g • unsaturated fat 14g
sodium 1582mg • calories 544

1 Heat the oil in a large pan, add the vegetables and garlic and fry over medium heat for about 5 minutes or until softened, stirring.

2 Add the wine, bouquet garni, mussels and salt and pepper. Cover the pan and cook over high heat for about 5 minutes or until the mussels are open, shaking the pan occasionally.

3 Lift the mussels out into four warmed soup plates, discarding any that are not open. Discard the bouquet garni. Add the stock to the pan and boil for 3–4 minutes until reduced. Add the butter and whisk until melted, then add the parsley. Check the seasoning and pour the sauce over the mussels.

127

PASTA

Quick to cook and immensely popular, pasta can be served as a

first course, or as a complete meal with the addition

of a simple salad and some crusty Italian or French bread.

SPAGHETTI WITH TOMATO SAUCE

The sauce can be prepared in advance and kept in the refrigerator for up to 1 week, or in the freezer for up to 3 months.

SERVES 6

500g dried spaghetti

leaves from 5 sprigs of fresh basil, shredded

freshly grated Parmesan cheese, to serve

FOR THE TOMATO SAUCE

2 tbsp olive oil

1 large Spanish onion, peeled and finely chopped

2 x 400g cans chopped tomatoes

2 tsp caster sugar

1 tsp dried oregano

1 bay leaf

salt and pepper

saturated fat 1g • unsaturated fat 5g
sodium 56mg • calories 373

1 First make the sauce: heat the oil in a medium pan until hot. Add the chopped onion and cook over low heat for about 10 minutes or until softened but not brown, stirring occasionally.

2 Add the tomatoes, sugar, oregano, bay leaf and salt and pepper to the pan. Stir well. Bring to the boil over high heat, then reduce the heat to low and simmer gently, uncovered, for about 30 minutes or until thickened, stirring occasionally.

3 Remove the bay leaf and taste the sauce to check seasoning. Keep hot over low heat while cooking the spaghetti (see below).

4 Drain the spaghetti into a colander, shake well, then return it to the empty pan in which it was cooked, or put it in a warmed large bowl.

5 Pour the tomato sauce over the spaghetti and toss to mix. Serve immediately, sprinkled with the fresh basil. Serve freshly grated Parmesan cheese separately in a small bowl.

VARIATION

TOMATO-CLAM SAUCE

Drain a 290g can baby clams in brine. Add the clams to the tomato sauce with the zested rind and juice of 1 lemon at the end of step 2. Heat through gently. Serve with lemon wedges rather than Parmesan.

COOKING SPAGHETTI

Cooking times vary with different brands, so check the packet for precise times. For more detailed information, see page 39.

Bring 4 litres water to the boil in a large pan. Add 1 tbsp salt.

Coil in the spaghetti, bring back to the boil and cook for 10–15 minutes.

CANNELLONI BOLOGNESE

*1 quantity Bolognese sauce
(see Master Recipe, page 82)*

*175g "no pre-cooking required"
dried cannelloni tubes*

a few gratings of nutmeg

salt and pepper

*600ml medium-consistency
hot white sauce (see page 68)*

50g Parmesan cheese, grated

saturated fat 22g • unsaturated fat 22g
sodium 554mg • calories 839

1 Simmer the Bolognese sauce
in a nonstick pan until no
excess liquid remains, stirring
constantly. Leave to cool.

2 Preheat the oven to 200°C
(fan oven 190°C), Gas 6.
Grease a baking dish measuring
about 25 x 20cm and 5cm deep.
Spread a little of the Bolognese
sauce in the bottom of the dish.

3 Use a small plastic bag to fill
the cannelloni tubes: cut a
corner from the sealed end of the
bag to make a 2cm opening. Put
2 large spoonfuls of the Bolognese
sauce into the bag at a time, and
squeeze into each tube.

4 Put the cannelloni tubes close
together in the dish, in a
single layer. Add the nutmeg and
salt and pepper to the white
sauce, then pour the sauce over
the cannelloni, making sure they
are covered. Top with the cheese.

5 Cover with foil and bake for
15 minutes, then remove the
foil and bake for 20 minutes
more or until golden brown.

PASTA PRIMAVERA

250g asparagus tips

*250g French beans, trimmed and
cut on the diagonal*

*1 courgette, trimmed
and cut into sticks*

salt and pepper

150g tub soft goat's cheese

*zested rind and juice of
1 small lemon*

2 tbsp olive oil

*1 large garlic clove, peeled
and crushed*

400g dried penne

saturated fat 5g • unsaturated fat 10g
sodium 189mg • calories 531

1 Plunge the vegetables into a
medium pan of salted boiling
water. Bring back to the boil and
boil for 2 minutes. Drain in a
colander, rinse in cold water and
shake well. Set aside.

2 Put the cheese in a saucepan
with the lemon rind and juice,
oil, garlic and salt and pepper. Stir
over low heat until the cheese has
melted, then add the vegetables
and mix well. Set aside.

3 Cook the penne in salted
boiling water for 10–15
minutes, or according to packet
instructions. Drain, turn into a
warmed large bowl and add the
vegetable mixture. Toss to mix.

VEGETABLE & NOODLE STIR-FRY

250g dried Chinese egg noodles

3 tbsp sunflower oil

*8 spring onions, sliced on the
diagonal into short lengths*

*2.5cm piece of fresh root ginger,
peeled and finely chopped*

*3 large garlic cloves, peeled and
very thinly sliced*

*1 large red pepper, cored,
deseeded and diced*

*225g baby button mushrooms,
trimmed and halved*

1 large egg, lightly beaten

dash of Tabasco sauce

salt and pepper

saturated fat 3g • unsaturated fat 14g
sodium 156mg • calories 408

1 Plunge the noodles into a
large pan of boiling water.
Remove from the heat, stir until
the noodles are separated, then
cover and let stand for
4–6 minutes. Drain in a colander
and shake well. Set aside.

2 Heat a wok over high heat for
1–2 minutes until very hot.
Add the oil and heat until it just
begins to smoke, then add the
spring onions and ginger and
stir-fry for 1 minute. Add the
garlic, red pepper and mushrooms
and stir-fry for 2 minutes.

3 Add the noodles and toss to
mix with the vegetables and
heat through. Pour in the beaten
egg, Tabasco and salt and pepper.
Stir and toss well so the egg coats
the noodles and vegetables. Taste
and add more Tabasco if you like.

STUFFED PASTA SHELLS

Make sure that the filled shells are completely covered in sauce before baking. Any uncovered shells will be chewy and tough.

1 quantity tomato sauce (see page 128)

12 large or 24 medium dried pasta shells

FOR THE FILLING

500g frozen leaf spinach, defrosted and well drained

250g carton mascarpone cheese

2 large eggs, lightly beaten

85g Parmesan cheese, grated

1 tbsp shredded fresh basil

a few gratings of nutmeg

salt and pepper

saturated fat 25g • unsaturated fat 19g sodium 389mg • calories 681

1 Purée the tomato sauce in the pan, using an electric hand-held blender with the blades held below the level of the sauce. Alternatively, purée the sauce in a food processor or blender, or work it through a sieve.

2 Make the filling: put the spinach and mascarpone in a bowl and beat together with a spoon. Add the eggs, Parmesan cheese, basil, nutmeg and salt and pepper. Beat well to mix.

3 Preheat the oven to 200°C (fan oven 190°C), Gas 6. Grease a baking dish measuring about 25 x 20cm and 5cm deep. Spread a little of the tomato sauce in the bottom of the dish.

4 Cook the pasta shells in salted boiling water for 10–15 minutes, or according to packet instructions. Drain in a colander. Fill the pan with cold water. Put the shells back into the pan.

5 Take the shells out of the water one at a time, drain and fill with the spinach mixture, then pack close together in the dish. Cover them with the remaining tomato sauce. Bake for 35 minutes or until bubbling.

MEAT LASAGNE

When using "no-precooking required" lasagne, the Bolognese and white sauces should be runny because this type of pasta absorbs a lot of liquid during baking.

1 quantity Bolognese sauce (see Master Recipe, page 82)

600ml medium-consistency hot white sauce (see page 68)

a few gratings of nutmeg

salt and pepper

50g Parmesan cheese, grated

about 6 sheets "no pre-cooking required" dried lasagne

saturated fat 22g • unsaturated fat 21g sodium 550mg • calories 772

1 Preheat the oven to 190°C (fan oven 180°C), Gas 5. Grease a baking dish measuring about 25 x 20cm and 5cm deep.

2 Spread one-third of the Bolognese sauce in the bottom of the dish. Add the nutmeg and salt and pepper to the white sauce, then spread one-third over the Bolognese.

3 Sprinkle with one-third of the cheese. Cover with a layer of lasagne sheets, not overlapping them. The dish will probably take 3 sheets, but you may have to break them to fit.

4 Repeat the layers of Bolognese sauce, white sauce, cheese and lasagne. Finish with layers of the remaining Bolognese, white sauce and cheese.

5 Bake the lasagne for about 30 minutes or until bubbling and golden brown.

VARIATION

LOW-FAT LASAGNE

Replace half the white sauce with a 250g carton low-fat curd cheese, and mix the two together well. Season with 1 heaped tsp Dijon mustard and extra salt and pepper, then use as the white sauce in the main recipe.

VEGETARIAN LASAGNE

500g frozen leaf spinach, defrosted and well drained

600ml medium-consistency hot white sauce (see page 68)

a few gratings of nutmeg

200g Emmental cheese, grated

about 6 sheets "no pre-cooking required" dried lasagne

FOR THE MUSHROOM SAUCE

2 tbsp olive oil

1 large onion, peeled and chopped

350g button mushrooms, trimmed and sliced

2 large garlic cloves, peeled and crushed

40g plain flour

400g can chopped tomatoes

1 tsp sugar

salt and pepper

1 tbsp shredded fresh basil

saturated fat 20g
unsaturated fat 17g
sodium 604mg
calories 668

1 First make the mushroom sauce: heat the oil in a nonstick sauté pan, add the onion and cook over medium heat for about 5 minutes or until just beginning to brown. Add the mushrooms and garlic, stir, then cook for about 5 minutes. Sprinkle in the flour and stir well.

2 Add the tomatoes, sugar and salt and pepper. Bring to the boil, then reduce the heat and simmer, uncovered, for about 15 minutes or until the sauce has reduced and thickened.

3 Preheat the oven to 190°C (fan oven 180°C), Gas 5. Grease a baking dish measuring about 25 x 20cm and 5cm deep.

4 Stir the basil into the mushroom sauce. Spread one-third in the bottom of the dish.

5 Scatter one-third of the spinach over the mushroom sauce, using your fingers. Season the white sauce with nutmeg and salt and pepper, spread one-third over the spinach in the dish, then sprinkle with one-third of the cheese.

6 Cover with a layer of lasagne sheets, not overlapping them. The dish will probably take 3 sheets, but you may have to break them to fit.

7 Repeat the layers of mushroom sauce, spinach, white sauce, cheese and lasagne. Finish with mushroom sauce, spinach, white sauce and cheese. Bake for about 30 minutes or until golden brown.

GRAINS & PULSES

Grains and pulses make nutritious main courses,

or can be used to create tasty and filling accompaniments to

grilled and pan-fried fish, poultry and meat.

SAFFRON RICE

60g butter

1 medium onion, peeled and chopped

225g arborio or risotto rice

850ml hot chicken stock

a large pinch of saffron threads

salt and pepper

40g Parmesan cheese, grated

saturated fat 11g • unsaturated fat 5g
sodium 416mg • calories 410

1 Melt half the butter in a medium pan. Add the onion and cook over medium heat for 5 minutes or until softened.

2 Add the rice and stir to coat with butter. Add a ladleful of stock; it will bubble and hiss. Stir until absorbed.

3 Add the saffron, salt and pepper, then a ladleful of stock. Stir until absorbed. If necessary, reduce the heat so the stock is just bubbling.

4 Add the remaining stock a ladleful at a time, stirring constantly, then continue to cook until the rice is creamy and al dente. The whole process should take 20–25 minutes. Stir in the remaining butter and Parmesan. Check the seasoning.

DHAL

250g red or orange lentils

600ml water

2.5cm piece of fresh root ginger, peeled and grated

1 large garlic clove, peeled and crushed

1 tsp ground turmeric

1½ tsp salt

FOR THE TOPPING

2 tbsp sunflower oil

1 tomato, cut into 8 wedges

1 onion, peeled and sliced

½ tsp dried chilli flakes

fresh coriander, to garnish

saturated fat 1g • unsaturated fat 7g
sodium 613mg • calories 283

1 Place the lentils, water, ginger, garlic, turmeric and salt in a medium pan. Bring to the boil, then reduce the heat and simmer for 20–30 minutes until soft.

2 Remove the pan from the heat and mash the lentils with a potato masher. Add a little hot water if the mixture is too thick. Keep hot.

3 Make the topping: heat the oil in a sauté pan until hot. Add the tomato, onion and chilli flakes and stir-fry over medium heat for about 2 minutes.

4 Transfer the dhal to a serving dish, top with the tomato and onion mixture and garnish with coriander. Serve immediately.

TABBOULEH

100g bulgar wheat

10 spring onions, chopped

1 small bunch of fresh parsley

10 fresh mint sprigs

3 tbsp lemon juice

3 tbsp olive oil

salt and pepper

saturated fat 2g • unsaturated fat 10g
sodium 8mg • calories 203

1 Place the bulgar in a bowl and cover generously with cold water. Let stand for 20–30 minutes. Drain the bulgar into a sieve, squeeze to remove excess water, then place in a bowl.

2 Finely chop the spring onions and herbs in a food processor, or by hand with a chef's knife, then add to the bulgar with the lemon juice, oil and salt and pepper. Stir well, cover and chill for about 2 hours before serving.

SUMMER COUSCOUS

1 vegetable stock cube

150g asparagus tips, cut into 2.5cm lengths

250g couscous

salt and pepper

juice of 1 lemon

3 tbsp olive oil

6 spring onions, chopped

150g mangetouts, sliced

50g pine nuts, toasted

3 tbsp each chopped fresh parsley and mint

lemon and mint, to garnish

saturated fat 2g
unsaturated fat 19g
sodium 432mg
calories 374

1 Crumble the stock cube into a medium pan, add 400ml boiling water and stir to dissolve. Bring to the boil, add the asparagus to the stock, cover and cook for 3 minutes.

2 Place the couscous in a large bowl. Set a colander over the bowl and pour in the stock and asparagus. When the stock has drained through, lift off the colander. Add salt and pepper to the couscous and stir well. Cover and leave to cool.

3 Run cold water over the asparagus to cool it quickly, then dry on kitchen paper.

4 Add the lemon juice and olive oil to the couscous and toss to mix.

5 Add the asparagus, spring onions, mangetouts, pine nuts and chopped herbs. Toss well, then check the seasoning. Serve at room temperature, topped with lemon and mint.

PAN-FRIES

For quick main dishes, pan-fries are perfect – food can be cooked in

a matter of minutes, and go straight from the pan to the table.

For best results, use a good-quality nonstick sauté pan.

GARLIC PRAWNS

16–20 raw tiger prawns in shells,
peeled and deveined

5 tbsp olive oil

3 garlic cloves, peeled
and crushed

salt and pepper

250ml tomato passata

juice of ½ lemon

1 tsp caster sugar

3 tbsp coarsely chopped
fresh parsley

zested rind of 1 lemon

saturated fat 3g • unsaturated fat 16g
sodium 416mg • calories 340

1 Place the prawns in a large bowl with the oil, garlic and salt and pepper. Toss well to mix.

2 Heat a large nonstick sauté pan over high heat for 2 minutes. Add the prawns with the oil and garlic and stir for 2 minutes or until pink. Reduce the heat to medium and add the passata, lemon juice and sugar. Cook, stirring, for 3–4 minutes. Check seasoning, then top with parsley and lemon zest.

HERB-CRUSTED FISH

75g fresh white breadcrumbs

2 tbsp chopped mixed fresh
tarragon, dill and chervil

zested rind of 1 lemon

4 pieces of haddock fillet, each
weighing 125–175g, skinned

salt and pepper

2 tbsp plain flour

1 large egg, beaten

2 tbsp olive oil

lemon wedges, to serve

saturated fat 2g • unsaturated fat 8g
sodium 286mg • calories 348

1 Process the breadcrumbs, herbs and lemon zest in a food processor until fine. For a coarser coating, just mix the ingredients together in a shallow dish.

2 Prepare each fillet in turn: sprinkle with salt and pepper, then coat with the flour and shake off the excess. Dip each piece in the beaten egg, then coat with the crumb mixture.

3 Heat the oil in a large nonstick sauté pan. Place the fish in the pan and cook over medium heat for 3 minutes on each side or until golden brown and crisp. Serve hot, with lemon wedges for squeezing.

TURKEY SEVILLE

4 turkey breast steaks

salt and pepper

2 tbsp olive oil

12 large fresh sage leaves

25g butter

4 tbsp sherry

150ml double cream

saturated fat 17g • unsaturated fat 18g
sodium 126mg • calories 492

1 Beat out the turkey breast steaks, then cut each one into three pieces. Sprinkle each piece with salt and pepper.

2 Heat the oil in a large nonstick sauté pan. Add the sage and fry over high heat until crisp. Remove from the pan and set aside.

3 Melt the butter in the pan until foaming. Add the turkey and pan-fry over high heat for 2 minutes on each side or until tender. Lift out into a serving dish and keep hot. Add the sherry and cream to the pan and bring to the boil, stirring. Check the seasoning, pour over the turkey and top with the sage leaves.

CAJUN-STYLE CHICKEN

2 tsp dried oregano

2 tsp sweet paprika

½ tsp ground ginger

½ tsp black pepper

¼ tsp cayenne pepper

1 tbsp olive oil

4 skinless boneless chicken breasts

salt

a few sprigs of thyme, to garnish

saturated fat 2g • unsaturated fat 5g
sodium 80mg • calories 173

1 Combine the oregano, spices and oil in a bowl, then rub over the chicken breasts to coat.

2 Heat a large nonstick sauté pan over high heat for 2 minutes. Add the chicken, smooth-side down, and pan-fry for 2–3 minutes until just beginning to blacken.

3 Turn the chicken over, reduce the heat and cook for 3–6 minutes until the juices run clear. Sprinkle with a little salt and the thyme just before serving.

VARIATION

CAJUN-STYLE SEA BASS

Substitute 4 thick steaks of sea bass, skinned, for the chicken. Coat with the same spicy mixture as for the chicken and pan-fry for 3 minutes on each side. Check to see whether the fish looks opaque all along the cut edge. If not, cook for a few seconds longer.

STIR-FRIES

Colourful and fresh-tasting, stir-fries are healthy and quick. A wok is the traditional pan for cooking, but if you haven't got one, a large nonstick sauté pan can be used – the deeper the sides the better.

SPICED SCALLOPS & PRAWNS

1 tbsp sunflower oil

2 large carrots, peeled and cut into thin sticks

400g raw tiger prawns in shells, peeled and deveined

200g queen scallops

6–8 spring onions, sliced

250ml coconut milk

1 tsp caster sugar

salt

fresh coriander leaves, to garnish

FOR THE SPICE MIX

3 garlic cloves, peeled

2.5cm piece of fresh root ginger, peeled

2 tsp mild curry powder

2 tbsp sunflower oil

saturated fat 9g • unsaturated fat 12g sodium 312mg • calories 368

1 First make the spice mix: put all the ingredients in a food processor fitted with the metal blade and process until smooth, or pound in a pestle and mortar.

2 Heat a wok over high heat for 1–2 minutes until very hot. Add the oil and heat until it just begins to smoke.

3 Reduce the heat to medium, add the carrots and stir-fry for 1 minute. Add the spice mix and stir-fry for 2 minutes. Add the prawns, scallops and onions and stir-fry over high heat for about 3 minutes until prawns are pink.

4 Add the coconut milk, sugar and salt. Stir and heat until bubbling. Garnish with coriander.

VEGETABLES WITH MARINATED TOFU

2 x 250g packets firm tofu

2 garlic cloves, peeled and finely chopped

2 tbsp finely chopped fresh thyme

1 tbsp sesame oil

salt and pepper

1 vegetable stock cube

2 tbsp sunflower oil

2 medium onions, peeled and thinly sliced

250g button mushrooms, trimmed and thinly sliced

300g cauliflower florets

300g broccoli florets

150ml dry white wine

1 tbsp cornflour

saturated fat 3g • unsaturated fat 15g sodium 447mg • calories 319

1 Drain and cube the tofu and place in a dish. Sprinkle the garlic, thyme, sesame oil and salt and pepper over the tofu. Cover and marinate for 20 minutes.

2 Dissolve the stock cube in 150ml boiling water. Heat a wok over high heat for 1–2 minutes until very hot. Add the tofu and marinade and stir-fry over medium heat until lightly browned. Transfer to a plate.

3 Heat the sunflower oil in the wok, add the onions and stir-fry for 3–4 minutes. Add the mushrooms, stir-fry for 2 minutes, then add the cauliflower and broccoli and stir-fry for 2 minutes. Pour in the wine and stock.

4 Blend the cornflour with 2 tbsp water, then make up to 100ml with more water. Pour into the wok, bring to the boil and stir-fry until the vegetables are tender. Add salt and pepper, then sprinkle the tofu over the top.

VARIATION

VEGETABLES WITH MARINATED STEAK

Substitute 2 fillet steaks (total weight about 300g) for the tofu and a beef stock cube for the vegetable stock cube. Cut the steaks into thin strips across the grain and stir-fry for 2–3 minutes.

HOISIN PORK

2 medium carrots

200g baby sweetcorn

4–6 spring onions

8 thin slices of lemon

3 tbsp sunflower oil

400g pork fillet, beaten out and sliced into thin strips

1 garlic clove, peeled and crushed

5 tbsp hoisin sauce

2 tbsp dry sherry

100g fresh beansprouts

fresh coriander, to garnish

saturated fat 4g
unsaturated fat 15g
sodium 1168mg
calories 348

1 Peel the carrots and cut into thin sticks. Cut the sweetcorn into 4cm lengths. Slice the spring onions on the diagonal. Cut the lemon slices into quarters.

2 Heat a wok over high heat for 1–2 minutes until very hot. Add 2 tbsp of the oil and heat until it just begins to smoke. Add the carrots, sweetcorn, spring onions and lemon and stir-fry over medium heat for 2 minutes or until the sweetcorn is tender.

3 Remove the vegetables with a slotted spoon. Add half the pork and stir-fry for 3 minutes. Remove with the slotted spoon. Heat the remaining oil in the wok, add the remaining pork and the garlic and stir-fry for 3 minutes.

4 Return the vegetables and pork to the wok, add the hoisin sauce and sherry and stir-fry until bubbling. Add the beansprouts and toss to mix. Serve hot, garnished with coriander.

CHAR-GRILLS

A ridged cast-iron pan like the one shown here is essential for char-grilling. It will enable you to cook quickly in the minimum amount of fat, and the food will be charred with attractive stripes.

VEGETABLES WITH SALSA VERDE

1 small aubergine

2 medium courgettes

4 medium peppers (2 red, 2 yellow)

1 large Spanish onion

1 tbsp olive oil

2 tsp balsamic vinegar

Parmesan cheese, to garnish

FOR THE SALSA VERDE

1 medium onion, peeled and finely chopped

2 tbsp chopped fresh parsley

2 tbsp shredded fresh basil

100ml olive oil

2 tbsp drained capers, finely chopped

salt and pepper

saturated fat 4g • unsaturated fat 29g sodium 66mg • calories 370

1 First make the salsa verde: place the onion, herbs, olive oil, capers and salt and pepper in a large bowl and mix together until well combined, then taste to check the seasoning. Cover the bowl with clingfilm and place in the refrigerator to chill the salsa while preparing and cooking the vegetables.

2 Trim the ends off the aubergine and cut lengthwise in half, then cut each half crosswise into 1cm slices and place in a bowl.

3 Trim the courgettes and cut into 1cm slices on the diagonal. Add to the bowl of aubergine slices.

4 Halve, core and deseed the peppers, then cut each half lengthwise into three wide strips. Trim away any white ribs so the strips will lie flat. Add to the bowl.

5 Peel the onion and cut it lengthwise into eight wedges. Add to the bowl, sprinkle in the olive oil and salt and pepper and toss well to mix all the ingredients together.

6 Preheat a char-grill pan over high heat for about 10 minutes. Reduce the heat to medium, then place the vegetables on the pan in batches, in a single layer. Cook for about 2 minutes on each side until they are lightly charred but still crisp. As each batch is cooked, transfer to a large bowl.

7 When all the vegetables are in the bowl, sprinkle with the balsamic vinegar and mix well. Arrange the vegetables on a large serving platter, spoon over the salsa and shave Parmesan cheese over the top. Serve warm or cold.

FRUITY PORK CHOPS

4 pork loin chops, excess fat removed

1 tbsp olive oil

salt and pepper

FOR THE FRESH FRUIT SALSA

75g raisins

1 dessert apple, finely chopped

1 orange, peeled and finely chopped

2 tbsp white or brown sugar

1 tbsp white wine vinegar

2 tbsp chopped fresh mint

saturated fat 3g • unsaturated fat 7g sodium 91mg • calories 286

1 First make the salsa: soak the raisins in boiling water for 10 minutes, drain and mix with the remaining ingredients. Chill.

2 Brush the chops with oil. Preheat a char-grill pan over high heat for about 10 minutes. Reduce the heat to medium, place the chops on the pan and cook for 5 minutes on each side or until the juices run clear when the meat is cut. Season, and serve with the salsa.

STEAK WITH ONION MARMELADE

The French term *marmelade* is used to describe fruit or vegetables that are cooked slowly until they are very soft. If you are serving wine with the meal, add a dash to the marmelade.

4 rump or sirloin steaks (125–175g each), fat snipped

1 tbsp olive oil

ONION MARMELADE

2 tbsp olive oil

3 large Spanish onions (700g), peeled and thinly sliced

1 tbsp chopped fresh thyme

salt and pepper

*saturated fat 7g • unsaturated fat 17g
sodium 89mg • calories 409*

1 First make the marmelade: heat the oil in a nonstick sauté pan, add the onions and cook over medium heat for 10 minutes or until softened but not browned, stirring often.

2 Turn the heat down to low and cover the pan. Continue to cook for 5–10 minutes or until the onions are very soft and pale golden, stirring from time to time. Add the thyme and salt and pepper, stir, re-cover and remove from the heat.

3 Preheat a char-grill pan over high heat for about 10 minutes.

4 Return the marmelade to the heat. Brush the steaks with olive oil. Reduce the heat to medium and place the steaks on the pan. Cook for 2 minutes, then turn the steaks over and cook for 3 minutes on the other side or until cooked to your liking (cut into one steak to see how the cooking is progressing).

5 Just before serving, sprinkle the steaks with salt and pepper and top with the onions.

GRILLS

Grilling preserves the natural flavour of food, and is one of the fastest

and easiest of cooking methods. No special equipment is required,

but no two grills are the same, so cooking times are approximate.

TANDOORI CHICKEN

4 skinless boneless
chicken breasts

FOR THE TANDOORI MARINADE

100ml plain yogurt

3 tbsp sunflower oil

2 tbsp cold water

1 small onion, peeled and grated

1 garlic clove, peeled and crushed

2 tsp ground ginger

1 tsp ground turmeric

1 tsp Madras (hot) curry powder

saturated fat 2g • unsaturated fat 6g
sodium 110mg • calories 195

1 Mix all the marinade ingredients together in a large bowl. Add the chicken breasts and turn to coat in the marinade. Cover the bowl with clingfilm and leave to marinate in the refrigerator for 8–24 hours.

2 Line the grill pan with foil and preheat the grill on high for about 5 minutes before cooking.

3 Drain the chicken breasts and arrange them on the grid of the grill pan. Reduce the grill heat to medium-high. Grill the chicken, about 10cm from the heat, for about 6 minutes on each side or until the juices are clear when the chicken is cut.

GRILLED TROUT

½ cucumber, peeled

40g butter

2 tbsp chopped fresh dill

juice of 1 lemon

salt and pepper

4 trout, each weighing
375–425g, boned

saturated fat 7g • unsaturated fat 9g
sodium 221mg • calories 385

1 Cut the cucumber lengthwise in half, scoop out the seeds with a spoon, then slice crosswise.

2 Melt half the butter in a saucepan. Add the cucumber, toss over low heat for 2 minutes, then remove from the heat and add the dill, lemon juice and salt and pepper. Stir to mix, then spread the cucumber out in a foil-lined grill pan. Preheat the grill 5 minutes before cooking.

3 Season the trout inside and out, then spread the remaining butter over the skin. Grill, about 10cm from the heat, for 4–7 minutes on each side until the flesh flakes easily when tested with a fork. Serve with the cucumber.

REAL BEEFBURGERS

Quantities given here are for two large burgers. If you prefer, shape the mixture into four smaller burgers. Serve in buns with a side salad.

SERVES 2

500g fine minced beef or
ground beef

1 small onion, peeled and
grated (optional)

salt and pepper

1–2 tbsp sunflower oil

saturated fat 10g • unsaturated fat 18g
sodium 166mg • calories 454

1 Place the meat in a bowl and add the onion if using. Add salt and pepper and mix lightly.

2 Form the mixture into two large burgers, using wet hands to stop the mixture sticking.

3 Line the grill pan with foil and preheat the grill for about 5 minutes before cooking.

4 Brush the burgers with oil on one side. Lay them, oiled-side down, on the grill and brush the tops with oil. Grill, about 10cm from the heat, for about 2–3 minutes on each side for rare burgers, 4–5 minutes for medium, 6 minutes for well-done.

SEAFOOD KEBABS

350g firm white fish fillet, such as monkfish, skinned

350g salmon fillet (thick end), skinned

8 raw tiger prawns in shells, peeled and deveined

6 baby courgettes, trimmed and each cut into 4 pieces

16 cherry tomatoes

FOR THE MARINADE

6 tbsp fruity olive oil

1 tbsp balsamic vinegar

3 tbsp chopped fresh tarragon or basil

2 large garlic cloves, peeled and crushed

salt and pepper

saturated fat 3g • unsaturated fat 15g
sodium 183mg • calories 341

1 First make the marinade: put all the ingredients in a large bowl and stir well to mix.

2 Cut the white fish and salmon into 16 equal-size chunks. Place in the marinade, add the prawns and mix. Cover and refrigerate for up to 6 hours.

3 Line the grill pan with foil. Just before cooking, preheat the grill for 5 minutes on high.

4 Lift the fish and prawns out of the marinade (reserve the marinade). Thread 2 chunks of each type of fish, 1 prawn, 3 pieces of courgette and 2 tomatoes on to each of eight skewers.

5 Arrange the skewers on the grid of the grill pan and brush with the marinade. Reduce the grill heat to medium-high. Grill the kebabs, about 10cm from the heat, for about 10 minutes, turning them twice and brushing with the marinade. Check that the fish is opaque in the centre.

6 Serve the fish and vegetables on the skewers on a large platter, or slide them off and serve them on individual plates.

CASSEROLES

These casseroles are all made in a single pan. Once they are simmering, they can be left unattended. You can prepare them the day before and the flavours will improve, but reheat thoroughly (see page 162).

CHICKEN CACCIATORE

The Italian word *cacciatore* means "hunter's style". Dishes with this name are usually rustic and homely, and often contain mushrooms. If you prefer, you can use 8 chicken thighs instead of 4 chicken legs.

2 tbsp olive oil

4 whole chicken legs, skinned

1 large onion, peeled and roughly chopped

2 green peppers, cored, deseeded and sliced

1 garlic clove, peeled and crushed

40g plain flour

200ml red wine

400g can chopped tomatoes

½ tsp granulated sugar

½ tsp dried oregano

salt and pepper

140g button mushrooms, trimmed and cut lengthwise into quarters

chopped fresh parsley, to garnish

*saturated fat 2g • unsaturated fat 8g
sodium 98mg • calories 257*

1 Preheat the oven to 160°C (fan oven 150°C), Gas 3. Heat the oil in a medium pan over medium heat. Add the chicken pieces and fry, turning them over occasionally with tongs, for about 10 minutes or until they are browned on all sides. Lift out the chicken and set aside on a plate.

2 Add the onion, peppers and garlic to the pan and cook for about 10 minutes or until softened, stirring occasionally.

3 Sprinkle the flour over the vegetables and stir for a few moments. Pour in the red wine, stir well and bring to the boil. Add the tomatoes with their juice, the sugar, oregano and salt and pepper. Bring back to the boil, stirring.

4 Return the chicken pieces to the pan and bring back to the boil, stirring, then cover and transfer to the oven. Cook for about 40 minutes, adding the mushrooms for the last 5 minutes. Stir the mushrooms into the sauce so they are covered.

5 Pierce the chicken with the tip of a knife to see if the juices run clear and the meat is tender, then check the seasoning of the sauce. Sprinkle liberally with chopped parsley just before serving.

VEGETABLE CURRY

750g mixed prepared vegetables (such as cauliflower, potatoes, carrots, leeks, French beans)

3 tbsp sunflower oil

2 medium onions, peeled and chopped

1 large garlic clove, peeled and crushed

2.5cm piece of fresh root ginger, peeled and finely chopped

1 tbsp garam masala

400g can chopped tomatoes

175ml pineapple juice

salt

*saturated fat 2g • unsaturated fat 11g
sodium 64mg • calories 247*

1 Cut the vegetables into pieces that are roughly similar in size so they cook evenly.

2 Heat the oil in a medium pan. Add the onions and fry over medium heat for 10 minutes or until browned, stirring often.

3 Add the garlic, ginger, garam masala, tomatoes, pineapple juice and salt and bring to a simmer, stirring. Add all of the vegetables, cover and cook over low heat for 15 minutes or until just tender. Check the seasoning.

MOROCCAN-STYLE SPICED LAMB

This casserole uses shoulder of lamb, which is well marbled with fat and has a very good flavour. If you like, prepare the dish a day ahead, cool, then chill in the refrigerator overnight. The next day, remove all the fat that has solidified on the surface, then reheat the casserole until bubbling before serving.

2 tbsp sunflower oil

1 large onion, peeled and finely chopped

750g–1kg boneless shoulder of lamb, trimmed and cut into 4cm cubes

½ tsp ground allspice

½ tsp ground ginger

25g plain flour

salt and pepper

500g (400ml) tomato passata

175g ready-to-use dried apricots, halved

7.5cm piece of cinnamon stick, broken crosswise in half

saffron rice (see page 132), to serve

1 tbsp sesame seeds

saturated fat 21g • unsaturated fat 28g sodium 291mg • calories 760

1 Heat the oil in a medium pan. Add the onion and cook over medium heat for 10 minutes or until golden, stirring occasionally.

2 Add the cubes of lamb to the pan, then sprinkle in the spices, flour and salt and pepper. Cook, stirring and turning the lamb, for 5 minutes or until the meat has lost its redness.

3 Pour the passata into a measuring jug and make up to 600ml with cold water. Pour on to the lamb, stirring, then add the apricots and cinnamon. Heat until a few bubbles appear, then cover and cook over low heat for 45 minutes.

4 Check from time to time to make sure the liquid is simmering very gently, with just the occasional bubble.

5 Uncover the pan and cook for a further 15 minutes or until the meat is tender enough to cut with the side of a fork. The cooking liquid should be thick enough to just coat the meat. Check the seasoning.

6 Spoon the stew on to a bed of saffron rice, removing the pieces of cinnamon as you come across them. Sprinkle with the sesame seeds just before serving.

ROASTS

A joint of roast meat is ideal for a special occasion, especially when you

can spare more time for preparation and cooking. Turn the

page to find accompaniments to serve with your chosen roast.

ROAST TURKEY WITH CHESTNUT STUFFING

If you can't get frozen chestnuts, use 120g dried chestnuts and soak them overnight in cold water.

SERVES 8–10

4–5kg turkey, defrosted if frozen

40g butter, at room temperature

FOR THE CHESTNUT STUFFING

100g streaky bacon rashers, rinds removed, diced

225g frozen chestnuts, defrosted and coarsely chopped

50g fresh white breadcrumbs

1 medium egg, beaten

½ bunch of watercress, trimmed and finely chopped

salt and pepper

*saturated fat 8g • unsaturated fat 10g
sodium 446mg • calories 460*

1 First make the stuffing: put the bacon in a nonstick sauté pan and cook over low heat until the fat runs. Add the chestnuts, cook over medium heat for 10 minutes or until the bacon is crisp, then add the breadcrumbs.

2 Transfer to a bowl and leave to cool. Add the egg, watercress and salt and pepper and mix well.

3 Preheat the oven to 180°C (fan oven 170°C), Gas 4. Spoon the cold stuffing into the neck end of the bird, pull the skin over and secure with a poultry pin. Twist the wing tips up and over; tie the wings and legs with string.

4 Spread the butter over the bird, sprinkle with salt and pepper, then place, breast-side up, on a rack in a roasting tin. If you have a meat thermometer, push it into the thickest part of a thigh, away from the bone.

5 Roast for 3–3½ hours until the juices run clear when a skewer is inserted into the thigh. If using a thermometer, the temperature should read 90°C. If the bird browns before it is cooked, cover with foil and continue roasting. Let rest, wrapped in foil, while making gravy (see page 103).

BEEF WELLINGTON

750g piece of thick end of beef fillet

25g butter, at room temperature

pepper

350g frozen puff pastry, defrosted

1 large egg, beaten

*saturated fat 17g • unsaturated fat 24g
sodium 416mg • calories 681*

1 Preheat the oven to 220°C (fan oven 200°C), Gas 7. Trim any fat or sinew from the beef, then place the meat in a small roasting tin. Spread the butter over the meat and sprinkle with pepper. Roast for 20 minutes for rare beef, 30 minutes for medium. Remove from the oven and leave to cool.

2 Roll out the pastry on a lightly floured surface to a rectangle three times wider than the beef and about 20cm longer.

3 Place the beef in the middle of the pastry. Bring the two long sides up over the beef to meet in the middle with a 2.5cm overlap. Brush the underside of the overlap with beaten egg and press to seal. Place the parcel seam-side down on a baking sheet, trim the ends of the pastry, leaving enough to fold underneath, and tuck edges under.

4 Brush the parcel with beaten egg. Roll the pastry trimmings into a long strip. Cut into thin strips and arrange in a criss-cross pattern on top of the parcel. The beef can be baked at this stage, or wrapped in clingfilm and kept in the refrigerator for up to 12 hours.

5 Preheat the oven to the same temperature as before. Brush pastry with beaten egg again and bake for 30 minutes. If the pastry browns too quickly, cover with foil. Serve cut into thick slices.

RACK OF LAMB WITH HERB CRUST

SERVES 4–6

1 large egg, beaten

2 racks of lamb (best end of neck), prepared and chined by the butcher, excess fat removed

40g fresh breadcrumbs

2 tbsp each finely chopped fresh parsley and mint

2 spring onions, finely chopped

1 garlic clove, peeled and crushed

zested rind of 1 lemon

salt and pepper

saturated fat 11g
unsaturated fat 11g
sodium 197mg
calories 385

1 Preheat the oven to 200°C (fan oven 190°C), Gas 6. Brush beaten egg over the fat on one side of each rack of lamb.

2 Combine the breadcrumbs, herbs, spring onions, garlic and lemon rind in a bowl. Add salt and pepper and 1 tbsp of the remaining beaten egg and mix together to form a wet paste.

3 Divide the paste in half, and spread one portion over the fat side of each rack.

4 Place the racks, herb-crust up, in a roasting tin, with the bones pointing towards the centre. Roast for 40–50 minutes for medium-rare (pink) meat, 1 hour for medium.

5 Remove from the oven, cover with foil and leave to rest in a warm place for 10 minutes before slicing into individual cutlets. If you like, serve with onion gravy (see pages 86–87).

ACCOMPANIMENTS

For a special occasion, serve one or two of these accompaniments

with roast meat or poultry. For boiled, mashed and roast

potatoes, see pages 60–61; for plain cooked vegetables, see page 161.

SAVOY CABBAGE STIR-FRY

If you like, use a heaped tablespoon of coarse-grain mustard instead of soy sauce.

2 tbsp olive oil

1 large onion, peeled and thinly sliced

2 garlic cloves, peeled and crushed

1 small Savoy cabbage, cored and finely shredded

2 tbsp light soy sauce

saturated fat 1g • unsaturated fat 7g
sodium 542mg • calories 123

1 Heat a wok or a large sauté pan over high heat for 1–2 minutes until very hot. Add 1 tbsp of the oil and heat until it just begins to smoke. Reduce the heat to medium, add the onion and garlic and stir-fry for about 2 minutes.

2 Add the remaining 1 tbsp oil to the wok, and then add the cabbage. Stir-fry for 2 minutes, then sprinkle the soy sauce over the vegetables and toss to mix.

YORKSHIRE PUDDING

SERVES 4–6

125g plain flour

2 large eggs

1 large egg yolk

250ml milk, either full cream or semi-skimmed

white vegetable fat

saturated fat 6g • unsaturated fat 8g
sodium 80mg • calories 270

1 Measure the flour into a bowl, make a well in the centre and add the eggs and the egg yolk. Whisk, gradually drawing in the flour from the sides of the bowl.

2 Continue whisking, pouring in the milk a little at a time and gradually drawing in all of the flour. Whisk until smooth. If time allows, cover the bowl and let the batter stand for about 30 minutes before cooking.

3 Preheat the oven to 220°C (fan oven 210°C), Gas 7. Put a little white vegetable fat in each hollow of a 12-hole Yorkshire pudding tin and heat in the oven for 10 minutes until very hot.

4 Remove the tin, give the batter a stir, then pour it into the hollows. Return to the oven and cook for 15 minutes until well-risen, golden and crisp.

BAKED FENNEL

6 small fennel bulbs

salt and pepper

1 tbsp olive oil

40g Parmesan cheese, grated

saturated fat 3g • unsaturated fat 4g
sodium 126mg • calories 97

1 Preheat the oven to 220°C (fan oven 210°C), Gas 7. Trim off the feathery tops and the ends of the fennel bulbs, leaving enough base for the layers of each bulb to hold together. Cut each one lengthwise in half.

2 Bring a medium pan of water to the boil. Add salt, then the fennel, and cook for 10–15 minutes or until almost tender. Drain well in a colander.

3 Place the fennel in a baking dish. Sprinkle with the oil and salt and pepper, and turn to coat. Spread the fennel halves out, cut-sides up, in the dish.

4 Sprinkle the Parmesan over the fennel. Bake for about 20 minutes or until the fennel is tender when tested with a skewer and the topping is golden brown.

GARLIC CREAM POTATOES

For a lighter version, replace the double cream with crème fraîche.

SERVES 4–6

900g medium potatoes, peeled

salt and pepper

300ml double cream

2 large garlic cloves, peeled and crushed

saturated fat 27g • unsaturated fat 15g
sodium 100mg • calories 561

1 Preheat the oven to 200°C (fan oven 190°C), Gas 6. Generously butter a baking dish measuring about 25 x 20cm and 5cm deep.

2 Cut the potatoes into slices about 3mm thick. Layer half the slices in the dish and sprinkle with salt and pepper. Pour the cream into a jug, then add the crushed garlic and mix well. Pour half this mixture evenly over the potatoes in the dish.

3 Cover with the remaining potato slices, layering them evenly. Sprinkle with salt and pepper, then pour over the rest of the garlic cream.

4 Cover the dish with buttered foil and bake for 30 minutes. Remove the foil and bake for about 50 minutes or until the potatoes are tender when pierced and the top is brown.

RATATOUILLE

If you like crunchy vegetables, reduce the cooking time by about half, and add the courgettes for the last 10 minutes only so that they retain their fresh green colour and firm texture.

4 tbsp fruity olive oil

1 large Spanish onion, peeled and sliced

1 large aubergine, sliced into rounds about 1cm thick

4 small courgettes (about 300g), trimmed and sliced

6 tomatoes, skinned, halved and deseeded

1 large red pepper, cored, deseeded and sliced

1 large garlic clove, peeled and crushed

1 tsp granulated sugar

salt and pepper

1 tbsp shredded fresh basil

saturated fat 2g • unsaturated fat 14g
sodium 13mg • calories 213

1 Heat the oil in a large nonstick sauté pan. Add the onion and cook over medium heat for about 10 minutes or until softened, stirring often.

2 Add the remaining vegetables, the garlic, sugar and salt and pepper. Stir well. Cover the pan and cook over low heat for about 45 minutes or until the vegetables are tender but still retain their shape. Stir gently from time to time. At the end of cooking, check the seasoning and sprinkle with the shredded basil.

SWEET & SOUR RED CABBAGE

Cooked this way, red cabbage will lose its bright colour and become a more mellow reddish-brown. It reheats very successfully, and can be made up to 2 days ahead.

900g hard red cabbage, cored and coarsely shredded

450g dessert apples, quartered, cored, peeled and sliced

250g onions, peeled and finely chopped

3 tbsp wine vinegar

3 tbsp soft light brown sugar

¼ tsp ground cinnamon

1 large garlic clove, peeled and crushed

salt and pepper

saturated fat 0g • unsaturated fat 1g
sodium 25mg • calories 153

1 Preheat the oven to 150°C (fan oven 140°C), Gas 2. Combine all the ingredients in a large ovenproof pan and bring to the boil on the hob, stirring well.

2 Cover and transfer to the oven. Cook for 2–2½ hours or until the cabbage is very tender, stirring once or twice. Once the cabbage is cooked, serve it immediately, or turn the oven off and leave the pan inside – the cabbage will retain its heat for up to 20 minutes.

SALADS

Packets of ready-prepared leaves from the supermarket are a

handy time-saver for the busy cook, but can become monotonous.

The following recipes will add interest to your salad repertoire.

MIXED LEAF SALAD

SERVES 4–6

4–6 spring onions, trimmed
and sliced

6 celery sticks, trimmed and cut
into diagonal slices 3mm wide

1 small fennel bulb, trimmed
and thinly sliced

4–6 tbsp French dressing
(see page 69)

½ cucumber

200g packet mixed salad leaves

1 Little Gem lettuce

about 20 leaves of rocket, baby
spinach or lamb's lettuce

salt and pepper

saturated fat 2g • unsaturated fat 11g
sodium 109mg • calories 148

1 Mix the onions, celery and
fennel in a large salad bowl.
Add the dressing and toss well.

2 Cut the cucumber lengthwise
in half, then cut across into
thick slices. Tear all the leaves
into manageable-size pieces.

3 Place half the cucumber and
half the leaves in the bowl.
Add salt and pepper, then the
remaining cucumber and leaves.
Season again. Cover and chill for
up to 4 hours. Toss before serving.

COLESLAW

½ white cabbage (about 325g)

4–6 tbsp French dressing
(see page 69)

½ small onion, peeled and
finely chopped

1 tsp Dijon mustard

salt and pepper

3 celery sticks

2 carrots

75–90ml mayonnaise

saturated fat 4g • unsaturated fat 26g
sodium 125mg • calories 324

1 Cut the cabbage lengthwise
into quarters, then remove the
core from each piece. Shred the
cabbage, either with a chef's
knife or in a food processor fitted
with the slicing disc.

2 Place the cabbage in a large
bowl and add the dressing,
onion, mustard and salt and
pepper. Toss to mix. Cover tightly
and chill for about 8 hours.

3 Trim the celery and slice
thinly on the diagonal. Peel
the carrots, then grate them
coarsely on a box grater or in a
food processor fitted with the
coarse-grating disc. Add to the
cabbage, toss to mix, then add the
mayonnaise and stir to combine.
Cover tightly and chill for 1 hour.
Check seasoning before serving.

SALAD DRESSINGS

Homemade dressings taste better than shop-bought ones. For
quantities of ingredients and further information, see page 69.

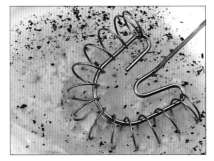

For French dressing, whisk wine vinegar,
olive oil and seasonings by hand.

For mayonnaise, work egg, sunflower oil
and seasonings in a food processor.

POTATO, APPLE & CELERY SALAD

750g new potatoes, scrubbed

salt and pepper

*120ml French dressing
(see page 69)*

2 dessert apples

juice of 1 lemon

*4 celery sticks, trimmed and cut
into slices 5mm thick*

*3 spring onions, trimmed
and shredded*

4 tbsp mayonnaise

chopped fresh parsley, to garnish

saturated fat 5g • unsaturated fat 30g
sodium 102mg • calories 480

1 Cook the potatoes in a pan
of salted boiling water for
15–20 minutes until tender.

2 Drain the potatoes, leave them
until cool enough to handle,
then cut in half. Place them in a
large bowl and sprinkle the
dressing over them. Leave to cool.

3 Quarter, core and dice the
unpeeled apples and place
them in a bowl. Pour the lemon
juice over the top and toss to
mix. This prevents discoloration.

4 Add the apples to the cold
potatoes with the celery,
onions and mayonnaise. Toss
well to mix. Check the seasoning
and sprinkle the salad with
parsley before serving.

FOUR BEAN SALAD

SERVES 6–8

400g can flageolet beans

432g can cannellini beans

420g can red kidney beans

420g can black eye beans

*6 tbsp French dressing
(see page 69)*

*1 large garlic clove, peeled
and crushed*

*4 celery sticks, trimmed and
cut into slices 5mm wide*

*1 medium red onion, peeled
and chopped*

salt and pepper

saturated fat 3g • unsaturated fat 19g
sodium 1402mg • calories 458

1 Drain all the beans in a
colander, then rinse them
under cold running water. Shake
well to drain. Line a baking tray
with a double thickness of
kitchen paper. Spread the beans
on the paper and shake the tray
until the beans are no longer wet.

2 Pour the dressing into a large
bowl, add the beans, garlic,
celery, onion and salt and pepper
and toss well. Cover and chill for
4 hours. Taste to check the
seasoning before serving.

VARIATION

BEAN SALAD WITH TUNA

Drain a 200g can tuna in oil and
break into large chunks. Fold into
the bean salad before chilling.
Garnish with 3 hard-boiled eggs,
shelled, cooled and quartered.

CAESAR SALAD

A classic Caesar salad includes
a raw or coddled egg, but
here mayonnaise is used instead.

*4 Little Gem lettuces, leaves
separated*

30g packet rocket leaves

*50g can anchovies in oil, drained
(optional)*

*croûtons made from 4 slices
of white bread*

*50g Parmesan cheese, grated
or in shavings*

FOR THE DRESSING

100ml mayonnaise

juice of ½ lemon

2 tsp Worcestershire sauce

1 garlic clove, peeled and crushed

1 tbsp olive oil

salt and pepper

saturated fat 8g • unsaturated fat 32g
sodium 825mg • calories 510

1 First make the dressing: put the
ingredients in a small bowl and
whisk to mix. Check seasoning.

2 Tear the lettuce and rocket
leaves into a large bowl. If
using anchovies, snip them into
small pieces over the bowl, using
scissors. Add the croûtons and
Parmesan cheese.

3 Pour the dressing over the
salad, toss well to mix and
serve immediately.

NIÇOISE SALAD

250g baby new potatoes, scrubbed

salt and pepper

250g French beans, trimmed and halved crosswise

1 garlic clove, peeled and crushed

1 tbsp chopped fresh parsley

1 tbsp shredded fresh basil

4 tbsp French dressing (see page 69), made without mustard

1 crisp lettuce, such as Cos or Little Gem

100g cherry tomatoes, halved

4 hard-boiled eggs, shelled, cooled and cut into wedges

2 x 200g cans tuna in oil, drained and broken into chunks

50–75g black olives in oil, drained

50g can anchovies in oil, drained

2–3 spring onions, trimmed and thinly sliced

saturated fat 5g • unsaturated fat 21g
sodium 989mg • calories 440

1 Cook the potatoes in a pan of salted boiling water for 15–20 minutes until tender.

2 Meanwhile, in another pan of salted boiling water, cook the French beans for about 3 minutes. Drain in a colander and rinse with cold water.

3 Drain the potatoes and leave them until they are cool enough to handle, then slice them. Leave to cool completely.

4 Add the garlic and herbs to the French dressing and whisk to mix. Check the seasoning.

5 Separate the lettuce leaves, then arrange them around the edges of four individual plates. Place the potatoes, tomatoes and eggs in the lettuce leaves, alternating them attractively.

6 Place the tuna in the centre, surround with the olives and arrange the anchovy fillets in a criss-cross pattern on top. Scatter with the spring onions and pour over the French dressing. Cover the salad loosely and chill in the refrigerator for about 1 hour before serving.

VARIATION

SALMON NIÇOISE

Replace the tuna with 4 small salmon fillets, chargrilled for 2 minutes on each side (see the Master Recipe on pages 92–93). Place 1 fillet in the centre of each plate, omit the anchovies and pour over the French dressing.

WARM CHICKEN LIVER SALAD

200g packet mixed
salad leaves

450g chicken livers

3 tbsp sunflower oil

6 streaky bacon rashers, rinds
removed, chopped

1 tbsp chopped fresh tarragon

4 tbsp French dressing
(see page 69), made
with coarse-grain mustard

croûtons made from
4 slices of white or brown bread

saturated fat 10g • unsaturated fat 37g
sodium 774mg • calories 640

1 Tear the salad leaves into manageable-size pieces. Place them in a large salad bowl, cover with clingfilm and chill in the refrigerator until ready to serve.

2 If using frozen chicken livers, defrost them thoroughly, then drain in a colander for about 10 minutes.

3 Trim the livers, then place them on a double thickness of kitchen paper to absorb excess liquid.

4 Heat the oil in a large nonstick sauté pan. Add the bacon and cook over low heat until the fat runs. Increase the heat to medium and fry until the bacon is browned and crisp. Remove with a slotted spoon and drain on kitchen paper.

5 Heat the oil and bacon fat remaining in the pan. Add the chicken livers and cook over high heat for no more than 3 minutes or until the livers are well browned but still a little pink inside.

6 Remove the pan from the heat. Add the tarragon and French dressing and swirl to mix with the livers.

7 Pour the hot livers and dressing over the crisp chilled salad leaves. Add the bacon and croûtons, toss together and serve immediately.

VARIATION

WARM CHICKEN & PINE NUT SALAD

Use 2 skinless boneless chicken breasts instead of the chicken livers, and cut them into thin strips on the diagonal. Pan-fry them as for the chicken livers in the main recipe; they will take about 3 minutes to cook through. Garnish with croûtons and about 40g pine nuts that have been tossed in a little olive oil over high heat for 1–2 minutes. Take care as they burn easily.

151

FRUIT DESSERTS

Of all desserts, fruit-based ones are the most popular. Fresh and colourful, they appeal even after the richest of main courses, and if you are serving a selection of desserts a fruity one is a must.

TROPICAL FRUIT SALAD

The sugar may be left out if the fruit is sweet and ripe.

SERVES 4–6

2 thin-skinned oranges

1 grapefruit

1 small ripe melon

1 small ripe pineapple

200g seedless black grapes, halved

50–75g caster sugar

saturated fat 0g • unsaturated fat 1g
sodium 63mg • calories 247

1 Peel and segment the oranges, working over a large bowl to catch the juice. Put the segments in the bowl. Segment the grapefruit and add to the oranges.

2 Cut the melon flesh into cubes. Add to the bowl. Peel and core the pineapple. Cut the flesh into chunks and add to the bowl. Add the grapes, sprinkle with sugar if using, and stir gently to mix. Cover and chill for 2 hours before serving.

MERINGUES WITH RASPBERRY COULIS

If you sandwich the meringues together ahead of time, they will be soft and squidgy. They can be prepared up to 5 hours ahead.

300ml whipping cream, chilled

8 meringues (see page 36)

200g raspberries

4 sprigs of fresh mint, to decorate

FOR THE SAUCE

200g raspberries

juice of ½ lemon

icing sugar, to taste

saturated fat 19g • unsaturated fat 10g
sodium 55mg • calories 400

1 First make the sauce: purée the raspberries in a food processor fitted with the metal blade. Rub the purée through a sieve to remove the seeds.

2 Add the lemon juice to the raspberry purée, then sweeten to taste with icing sugar. Cover and chill until ready to serve.

3 Whip the cream until it is thick. Sandwich the meringues together in pairs with the cream in the middle.

4 Spoon the raspberry sauce in a pool on each of four dessert plates. Place a pair of meringues on each pool of sauce and dust with icing sugar. Divide the raspberries between the plates and decorate with mint sprigs.

SEGMENTING AN ORANGE

Thin-skinned oranges have the most juice, so they are a good choice for a fruit salad. For more detailed information, see page 64.

Stand the orange upright and cut away its peel following the contours of the fruit.

Cut down between both sides of each membrane to release the orange segments.

ORANGE PASSION

This dessert can be prepared up to the end of step 2, then kept covered in the refrigerator for up to 10 hours. For a special occasion, sprinkle the oranges with brandy or Grand Marnier.

3 large thin-skinned oranges

90g light soft brown sugar

150g tub half-fat crème fraîche

150g tub plain Greek yogurt

saturated fat 6g • unsaturated fat 3g
sodium 69mg • calories 254

1 Peel the oranges, then slice them crosswise into rounds. Divide the orange slices equally among four stemmed glasses or ramekins. Sprinkle with the juice from the oranges, then sprinkle each portion with 1 tsp sugar.

2 Combine the crème fraîche and yogurt in a small bowl. Spoon on top of the oranges.

3 Sprinkle the remaining sugar evenly over the cream topping. Chill in the refrigerator for 2 hours before serving.

VARIATION

MANGO PASSION

Use 1 large ripe mango instead of the oranges. Cut the mango vertically along one side of the stone, then repeat on the opposite side to make three pieces. Cut away the flesh from all sides of the piece with the stone in. Remove the skin, then chop the flesh and divide it equally among the glasses or ramekins. Continue as in the main recipe.

LEMON & LIME CHEESECAKE

SERVES 4–6

FOR THE CRUMB CRUST

10 digestive biscuits, crushed

50g butter, melted

25g demerara sugar

FOR THE FILLING

150ml double cream

397g can condensed milk

175g low-fat cream cheese, at room temperature

zested rind and juice of 2 large lemons

zested rind and juice of 1½ limes

TO DECORATE

150ml whipping cream, chilled

½ lime, thinly sliced

saturated fat 25g • unsaturated fat 16g
sodium 471mg • calories 668

1 First make the crust: put the ingredients in a bowl and stir until mixed. Turn out into a 20cm loose-bottomed quiche tin and press firmly and evenly over the bottom and up the sides using the back of a metal spoon. Chill for 30 minutes until set.

2 Make the filling: place the double cream, condensed milk and cream cheese in a bowl with the lemon and lime rinds. Mix thoroughly. Using a balloon whisk, gradually whisk in the lemon and lime juices and continue whisking until the mixture thickens.

3 Pour the lemon and lime filling into the crumb crust and spread it evenly. Cover and chill overnight.

4 Up to 6 hours before serving, whip the cream until it just holds its shape. Decorate the top of the cheesecake with swirls of whipped cream and slices of lime, then return to the refrigerator.

BAKED APPLES

4 large cooking apples

50g light soft brown sugar

50g butter

2 tbsp water

saturated fat 7g • unsaturated fat 4g
sodium 98mg • calories 219

1 Preheat the oven to 180°C (fan oven 170°C), Gas 4. Core the apples whole, then make a slit in the skin around the circumference of each apple (this will prevent the apples from bursting). Place the apples in a baking dish.

2 Fill the hollow centres of the apples with the sugar, and put a knob of butter on top of each one. Pour the water into the dish. Bake for 35–40 minutes or until the apples are soft and puffy. The sugar, butter and water will make a syrupy sauce to spoon over the apples. Serve hot, with cream or vanilla ice-cream.

VARIATION

SPICED APPLES

Fill the centres of the apples with 100g raisins, 75g demerara sugar and ¼ tsp ground cinnamon. Cook as for baked apples.

PLUM CRUMBLE WITH HAZELNUTS

750g plums, halved and stoned

40g granulated sugar

2 tbsp water

FOR THE CRUMBLE TOPPING

225g plain flour

100g butter, cubed

40g granulated sugar

100g toasted hazelnuts, chopped

saturated fat 15g • unsaturated fat 21g
sodium 194mg • calories 680

1 Preheat the oven to 180°C (fan oven 170°C), Gas 4. Put the plums in a baking dish measuring about 25 x 20cm and 5cm deep. Sprinkle the fruit with the sugar and water.

2 Make the crumble topping: place the flour in a bowl and add the butter. Rub the butter into the flour until the mixture looks like breadcrumbs. Stir in the sugar and hazelnuts.

3 Scatter the crumble topping evenly over the fruit. Bake for 45 minutes or until the topping is golden brown and the fruit juices are bubbling. Test the plums with a skewer to see if they are tender; if not, cover the crumble with foil and bake for a further 10–15 minutes. Serve warm with cream or custard (see page 68).

VARIATION

APRICOT CRUMBLE

Omit the hazelnuts. Use apricots instead of plums and soft brown sugar instead of white sugar. If you like, use half wholemeal and half white flour.

LEMON & APPLE TART

Baking the tart on a preheated baking sheet ensures that the bottom of the pastry case will be crisp, not soggy.

SERVES 4–6

20cm uncooked pastry case in its tin (see pages 66–67)

FOR THE FILLING

2 large eggs

100g caster sugar

zested rind and juice of 1 lemon

50g butter, melted

1 large cooking apple (about 300g)

saturated fat 16g • unsaturated fat 15g
sodium 314mg • calories 568

1 Place a baking sheet in the oven and preheat to 200°C (fan oven 190°C), Gas 6.

2 Make the filling: put the eggs and sugar in a bowl with the lemon rind and juice. Stir until evenly blended. Add the melted butter and stir to mix.

3 Peel and core the apple, then coarsely grate it directly into the bowl that contains the filling mixture. Stir well, then pour the filling into the pastry case.

4 Set the tart in its tin on the hot baking sheet and bake for 40 minutes or until the pastry is golden brown and the filling is slightly risen and browned. If the tart browns too much before the end of the cooking time, cover it loosely with foil and continue to cook. Serve warm.

PINEAPPLE & GINGER PAVLOVA

3 large egg whites

175g caster sugar

1 tsp vinegar

1 tsp cornflour

300ml whipping cream, whipped

200g can pineapple chunks in natural juice, drained

50g stem ginger in syrup, drained and finely chopped

saturated fat 19g • unsaturated fat 10g
sodium 116mg • calories 513

1 Preheat the oven to 160°C (fan oven 150°C), Gas 3. Line a baking sheet with nonstick baking parchment and mark a 20cm circle on it.

2 Place the egg whites in a clean and dry large bowl. Using an electric mixer on full speed, whisk the egg whites until they stand in stiff peaks.

3 Add the sugar 1 tsp at a time, continuing to whisk on full speed until the whites are glossy. Blend the vinegar and cornflour together and whisk into the whites with the last spoonful of sugar.

4 Spoon the meringue on to the circle on the paper, and spread it so that the edge is slightly higher than the centre. Place in the oven, turn the temperature down to 150°C (fan oven 140°C), Gas 2, and bake for 1 hour.

5 Turn the oven off and let the pavlova go cold in the oven. Transfer to a platter, spoon the cream in the centre and top with the pineapple and ginger.

PINEAPPLE UPSIDE-DOWN PUDDING

60g butter

60g light soft brown sugar

5 canned pineapple rings in natural juice

15 glacé cherries

FOR THE SPONGE

125g soft baking margarine

125g caster sugar

175g self-raising flour

1 tsp baking powder

2 large eggs

saturated fat 17g • unsaturated fat 23g
sodium 656mg • calories 765

1 Preheat the oven to 180°C (fan oven 170°C), Gas 4. Grease a 20cm springform tin and line the base with greaseproof paper. Melt the butter, pour it into the tin and sprinkle with the sugar.

2 Drain the pineapple, reserving the juice. Arrange the rings in the tin, cutting them to fit as shown. Place the glacé cherries in the centre of the pineapple rings and between them.

3 Make the sponge: place the margarine, sugar, flour, baking powder and eggs in a large bowl. Add 2 tbsp pineapple juice. Beat with an electric mixer on slow speed for 2 minutes, or with a wooden spoon for 3–4 minutes.

4 When the mixture is soft enough to drop off the beaters or spoon, it is ready for baking. If necessary, add a few more drops of pineapple juice.

5 Spoon the sponge mixture over the fruit in the tin and spread it out evenly, taking care not to dislodge the arrangement of fruit. Bake for about 45 minutes or until the sponge is risen and springy to the touch. If the sponge browns too much before the cooking time is completed, cover loosely with foil.

6 Hold a warmed plate upside down over the tin and turn the two over together so the pudding inverts on to the plate.

CAKES & COOKIES

Homemade bakes are usually reserved for special occasions, so you need to be sure of success every time. Here is a small selection of tried and tested recipes that you can turn to again and again.

EASY FRUIT CAKE

This recipe makes a kind of fruit bread, ideal for picnics and packed lunches as well as a teatime treat. If you wrap it tightly in greaseproof paper, it will keep in an airtight tin for up to 2 weeks.

CUTS INTO 12 SLICES

225g soft baking margarine

225g caster sugar

4 large eggs

225g self-raising flour

100g ground almonds

½ tsp almond extract

450g mixed dried fruit

25g flaked almonds (optional)

saturated fat 6g • unsaturated fat 16g
sodium 268mg • calories 458

1 Preheat the oven to 160°C (fan oven 140°C), Gas 3. Grease a 20cm springform cake tin. Line the base with greaseproof paper, then grease the paper.

2 Place all the ingredients, except the dried fruit and the almonds, in a large bowl. Beat with an electric mixer for 2–3 minutes, or with a wooden spoon for a little longer, until thoroughly mixed. Add the dried fruit and stir in with a wooden spoon.

3 Turn the mixture into the tin and smooth the top. If you like, sprinkle with the almonds. Bake for 1½–2 hours. To test for doneness, insert a skewer in the centre of the cake: when withdrawn, it should be clean and dry, not wet or sticky. Leave the cake to cool in the tin.

CHOCOLATE BROWNIES

This very easy, one-stage recipe makes brownies with a soft, cakey texture.

MAKES 12

225g soft baking margarine

350g light soft brown sugar

4 large eggs

50g cocoa powder, sifted

250g self-raising flour

½ tsp baking powder

85g walnut pieces (optional)

FOR THE FROSTING

3 tbsp cocoa powder, sifted

25g unsalted butter, at room temperature, cubed

4 tbsp boiling water

225g icing sugar, sifted

saturated fat 8g • unsaturated fat 13g
sodium 369mg • calories 469

1 Preheat the oven to 180°C (fan oven 160°C), Gas 4. Grease a traybake tin measuring 30 x 23cm, line the base with greaseproof paper, then grease the paper.

2 Place the margarine, sugar, eggs, cocoa powder, flour and baking powder in a large bowl. Beat with an electric mixer on low speed for about 3 minutes, or with a wooden spoon for a little longer, until smooth. Stir in the walnuts, if using.

3 Pour the mixture into the tin, spread evenly, then bake for 40–45 minutes, covering with foil for the last 10 minutes. Test with a skewer (see Easy Fruit Cake, left). Leave to cool in the tin until warm, then turn out on to a rack and cool completely.

4 Make the frosting: place the cocoa powder and butter in a bowl and gradually stir in the boiling water until smooth. Stir in the icing sugar. Leave to cool.

5 Spread the frosting evenly over the brownie base with a palette knife. Leave to set, then cut into 12 x 7.5cm squares.

BLUEBERRY MUFFINS

MAKES 12

2 large eggs

85g granulated sugar

225ml milk

100g butter, melted and cooled a little

1 tsp vanilla extract

zested rind of 1 lemon

280g self-raising flour

1 tsp baking powder

225g blueberries

saturated fat 5g • unsaturated fat 2g
sodium 211mg • calories 200

1 Preheat the oven to 200°C (fan oven 190°C), Gas 6. Line each hollow of a 12-hole muffin tin with a paper case.

2 Place the eggs in a large bowl, add the sugar, milk, melted butter, vanilla extract and lemon rind and stir to combine. Sift the flour and baking powder into the bowl. Fold the ingredients together very roughly: this should not take more than 20 strokes, and the mixture should still look lumpy and uneven. Add the blueberries and stir them in.

3 Divide the mixture equally between the 12 paper cases, dropping it in from the tip of a spoon. Bake for 25–30 minutes or until the muffins are well risen and splitting a little across the top. Transfer to a rack. Leave to cool slightly but serve warm.

CHOCOLATE-CHIP COOKIES

MAKES 24

85g soft baking margarine

100g caster sugar

1 large egg

175g self-raising flour

½ tsp vanilla extract

50g plain chocolate chips

50g chopped nuts

saturated fat 2g • unsaturated fat 3g
sodium 65mg • calories 94

1 Preheat the oven to 180°C (fan oven 170°C), Gas 4. Grease a baking sheet.

2 Place the margarine, sugar, egg, flour and vanilla extract in a large bowl. Beat with an electric mixer for 2 minutes, or with a wooden spoon for a little longer, until smooth. Stir in the chocolate and nuts.

3 Divide the mixture into thirds (each third should yield 8 cookies). Use two teaspoons to scoop the mixture from the bowl and drop it on to the baking sheet. If you space the mounds about 7.5cm apart, you will probably get 8 on the sheet at a time. With the back of a spoon, flatten each mound into a round about 5cm in diameter.

4 Bake for 15–20 minutes or until pale golden brown with slightly darker edges. The cookies will be only just firm to the touch. Lift carefully off the baking sheet with a palette knife and transfer to a rack to cool. Wipe the sheet, let it cool and grease it again before baking the next batch.

LEMON SLICES

MAKES 16

225g soft baking margarine

225g caster sugar

275g self-raising flour

2 tsp baking powder

4 large eggs

4 tbsp milk

zested rind of 2 lemons

FOR THE GLACÉ ICING

225g icing sugar, sifted

3 tbsp lemon juice

saturated fat 4g • unsaturated fat 8g
sodium 242mg • calories 297

1 Preheat the oven to 180°C (fan oven 160°C), Gas 4. Grease a traybake tin measuring 30 x 23cm, line the base with greaseproof paper, then grease the paper.

2 Place all the cake ingredients in a large bowl. Beat with an electric mixer for 1–2 minutes, or with a wooden spoon for a little longer, until smooth. Turn into the tin and spread evenly.

3 Bake for 35–40 minutes or until risen and springy to the touch. Run a knife around the edge of the cake to loosen it from the tin, then turn it out on to a rack and leave to cool.

4 Make the icing: stir the sugar and lemon juice together until smooth. Spread over the cake, leave to set, then cut into slices.

BREAD

Making bread and pizza is a most satisfying task. Remember

to choose a day when you know you will be at home

to keep an eye on the rising. There is very little else to do.

FARMHOUSE LOAF

500g strong white flour

2 tsp salt

6g sachet fast-action dried yeast

300ml tepid water

1 tbsp plus 1 tsp sunflower oil

*saturated fat 3g • unsaturated fat 22g
sodium 3126mg • calories 1895*

1 Measure the flour, salt and yeast into a large bowl. Pour in the water and 1 tbsp oil and mix to a soft dough. Add 2–3 tsp more tepid water if necessary.

2 Turn the dough out on to a lightly floured surface and knead for 10 minutes.

3 Rub 1 tsp oil round a large bowl. Turn the dough in the bowl to coat in the oil, then cover the bowl with clingfilm. Leave in a warm place for about 1½ hours or until doubled in size.

4 Grease a 20 x 10.5cm loaf tin. Turn the dough on to the work surface and pat or roll it into a 20 x 18cm rectangle.

5 Roll up the dough from one long side. With the seam underneath, drop it into the tin. Cover loosely with clingfilm and leave to rise in a warm place for about 30 minutes or until risen 2.5–3cm above the edges of tin.

6 Preheat the oven to 230°C (fan oven 220°C), Gas 8. Bake the loaf for 10 minutes, then lower the heat to 200°C (fan oven 190°C), Gas 6 for a further 30–40 minutes or until golden brown. Turn the loaf out of the tin and tap it on the bottom: it should sound hollow. If not, place it upside down in the oven for a few minutes more. Cool on a rack.

VARIATIONS

OLIVE BREAD

Make the dough as in steps 1–3 of the main recipe, but replace the sunflower oil with fruity olive oil. In step 4, work in 100g black and green olives, stoned and chopped, kneading them firmly into the dough until they are evenly distributed. Continue as in the main recipe.

SUN-DRIED TOMATO BREAD

Drain 100g sun-dried tomatoes in olive oil, reserving the oil. Chop the tomatoes roughly. Make the dough as in steps 1–3 of the main recipe, using the oil from the tomatoes instead of sunflower oil. In step 4, work in the chopped tomatoes, kneading them firmly into the dough until they are evenly distributed. Continue as in the main recipe.

ANCHOVY PIZZA

MAKES 2

250g strong white flour

1 tsp salt

½ x 6g sachet fast-action dried yeast

150ml tepid water

1 tbsp plus 1 tsp fruity olive oil

FOR THE TOPPING

150g packet mozzarella cheese

50g can anchovies in oil

6 tbsp sun-dried tomato paste

6 stoned black olives, halved

2 tbsp fruity olive oil

½ tsp dried oregano

*saturated fat 14g • unsaturated fat 35g
sodium 2039mg • calories 1007*

1 Measure the flour, salt and yeast into a large bowl. Pour in the water and 1 tbsp oil and mix to a soft dough. Add 2–3 tsp more tepid water if necessary.

2 Turn the dough out on to a lightly floured surface and knead for 10 minutes.

3 Rub remaining oil round bowl. Turn the dough in the oil, then cover bowl with clingfilm. Leave in a warm place for about 1½ hours or until doubled in size.

4 Grease two baking sheets. Knead the dough for a few minutes, then divide in half. Press each piece into a 23–25cm round on a baking sheet, pulling the edges of the dough up so that they form a rim.

5 Drain the mozzarella and slice thinly. Drain the anchovies. Spread the tomato paste over each pizza, then top with the mozzarella, anchovies and olives, arranging them carefully. Sprinkle with the oil and oregano. Set aside to rest.

6 Preheat the oven to 230°C (fan oven 220°C), Gas 8. Bake for about 10 minutes or until the pizza edges are crisp and golden, swapping the sheets over halfway.

VARIATIONS

PEPPERONI PIZZA

Make the pizza bases as in steps 1–4 of the main recipe, then spread with the tomato paste and top with the mozzarella as in step 5. Arrange 50g pepperoni, thinly sliced, over the mozzarella and sprinkle with 25g grated Parmesan cheese and 2 tbsp sliced pickled mild chillies. Continue as in the main recipe.

TUNA PIZZA

Make the pizza bases as in steps 1–4 of the main recipe, then spread with the tomato paste as in step 5. Drain and flake a 200g can tuna in oil, then spread it over the tomato paste. Sprinkle with 1 tbsp capers, drained and chopped, 50g mozzarella cheese, thinly sliced, ½ tsp dried oregano and salt and pepper. Continue as in the main recipe.

COOK'S NOTES

These charts provide at-a-glance cooking times and temperatures to help you when you are cooking. On the following pages you will find information on food safety and conversion tables.

USING A THERMOMETER

When roasting meat or poultry, a meat thermometer will register the internal temperature – this is the most accurate way to gauge the degree of doneness. At the start of cooking, insert the probe of the thermometer into the thickest, lean part of the meat, away from the bone. Check the temperature on the dial towards the end of cooking to see if it corresponds to the one given below.

MEAT	TEMPERATURE
LAMB	
medium-rare	70–75°C
well-done	80°C
BEEF	
rare	60–65°C
medium	70°C
well-done	75°C
PORK	
well-done	90°C
POULTRY	
cooked through	90°C

DEFROSTING POULTRY

All frozen poultry must be thoroughly defrosted before cooking, or it will not cook through. For birds up to 1.8kg, defrost in a cold place overnight, or in the refrigerator for 36 hours. Birds over 1.8kg need about 15 hours in a cold place or 48 hours in the refrigerator. Check that no ice crystals remain in the cavity before cooking.

USING A FAN OVEN

Lower the temperatures given in the charts by 10–20°C, according to your oven manufacturer's handbook.

ROASTING MEAT

TYPE	SIZE	OVEN	TIME
BEEF			
rib/sirloin	2.25–2.5kg	200°C/Gas 6	1½–1¾ hours (rare)
			2–2¼ hours (medium)
			2½–2¾ hours (well-done)
topside	1–2kg	180°C/Gas 4	1–1½ hours (rare)
			1¾–2 hours (medium)
			2¼–2½ hours (well-done)
fillet (thick end)	1kg	220°C/Gas 7	30 minutes (medium-rare)
	2kg		40 minutes (medium-rare)
LAMB			
whole leg/whole shoulder	1.5–2.5kg	180°C/Gas 4	1½–2¼ hours (medium-rare)
			1¾–2½ hours (well-done)
half leg/half shoulder	1–1.6kg	180°C/Gas 4	1–1¾ hours (medium-rare)
			1½–2 hours (well-done)
PORK			
loin or shoulder (boned and rolled)	1–1.5kg	180°C/Gas 4, then 220°C/Gas 7	1¾–2¼ hours (220°C/Gas 7 for last 20 minutes)
	2–2.5kg	180°C/Gas 4, then 220°C/Gas 7	2½–3 hours (220°C/Gas 7 for last 20 minutes)

ROASTING POULTRY

BIRD	SIZE	OVEN	TIME
CHICKEN	1.5–1.8kg	200°C/Gas 6	1¼–1½ hours
	2.5–3kg	200°C/Gas 6	2–2¼ hours
DUCK	1.8kg	200°C/Gas 6, then 180°C/Gas 4	45 minutes, then 1½ hours
	2.5kg	200°C/Gas 6, then 180°C/Gas 4	45 minutes, then 2 hours
TURKEY	4–5kg	180°C/Gas 4	3–3½ hours
	6–8kg	180°C/Gas 4	4–4¾ hours

GREEN VEGETABLES

■ For green vegetables with a good colour, crisp bite and maximum nutrients, cook for the minimum time in the minimum amount of water. Do not cover the pan.
■ Bring the water to the boil in a pan, add salt, then the vegetables. Start timing the moment the water returns to the boil. When the time is up, drain the vegetables in a colander. The times given here are approximate: they will vary according to the size and age of the vegetable.

BOILING GREEN VEGETABLES	
TYPE	APPROXIMATE TIME
Beans, broad, shelled	6 minutes
Beans, French, whole	6 minutes
Beans, runner, sliced	5 minutes
Broccoli (calabrese), florets	6 minutes
Brussels sprouts, whole	6 minutes
Cabbage, leafy, shredded	3 minutes
Cauliflower, florets	6 minutes
Mangetouts	2 minutes
Peas, shelled	3 minutes
Sugarsnaps	2 minutes

ROOT VEGETABLES & SQUASH

■ Root vegetables should always be cooked in a covered pan – they are grown in the dark, underground, and so they are cooked in the dark. Acorn squash, pattypan squash and pumpkin are cooked in the same way.
■ Put the vegetables in a saucepan, add enough cold water to cover them, then add salt. Cover the pan, bring to the boil and start timing from this moment. When the time is up, drain the vegetables in a colander.

BOILING ROOT VEGETABLES & SQUASH	
TYPE	TIME
Acorn squash, cut into chunks	15–20 minutes
Carrots, sliced/sticks	2–3 minutes
Carrots, whole young	6 minutes
Parsnips, cut into chunks	15–20 minutes
Pattypan squash, whole	6 minutes
Potatoes, cut into chunks	15–20 minutes
Potatoes, whole new	15–20 minutes
Pumpkin, cut into chunks	15–20 minutes
Swede, cut into chunks	15–20 minutes
Turnips, cut into chunks	10 minutes

PASTA & RICE

■ Timings for pasta and rice depend on individual varieties and brands, so always check the packet for precise instructions. Test both pasta and rice just before the end of the recommended cooking times to make sure they do not overcook. For detailed information on cooking methods, see pages 38–39.

BOILING RICE & PASTA	
TYPE	TIME
RICE Basmati	10–15 minutes
Brown long-grain	20–30 minutes
White long-grain	12–15 minutes
PASTA Dried	10–15 minutes
Dried Chinese egg noodles	6 minutes (soaking)
Fresh	2–3 minutes

PULSES

■ All pulses, except lentils, need soaking overnight before cooking.
■ At the start of cooking, always boil beans and peas rapidly for 10 minutes to destroy any toxins they may contain. For detailed information on cooking methods, see page 41.

BOILING PULSES	
TYPE	TIME
Aduki beans	45 minutes
Black beans	1–1½ hours
Borlotti beans	1–1½ hours
Cannellini beans	1–1½ hours
Chickpeas	2 hours
Lentils	20–30 minutes
Red kidney beans	1¼ hours
Split peas	2 hours

FOOD SAFETY

IT IS IMPORTANT to handle and store perishable foods with care, so they can be enjoyed at their best, and to help prevent food poisoning. Buy from a reputable retailer, first checking the "sell-by" and "use-by" dates. Take fresh food home and put it in the refrigerator or freezer as soon as possible. Keep work surfaces, utensils and hands clean. Separate chopping boards should be kept for raw and cooked foods, but if this is not possible, wash boards thoroughly in between each use. These guidelines are a matter of commonsense and apply to all fresh food, but some foods need special care – these are dealt with below.

CHEESE
■ Cheeses made from unpasteurized milk, especially soft cheeses, soft mature cheeses (pasteurized and unpasteurized), and blue-veined cheeses, should not be eaten by pregnant women, babies, young children, the sick and the elderly. These people are at greater risk from the listeria bacteria which may be present in these cheeses.

EGGS
■ Always buy fresh eggs from a reputable retailer, first checking that the shells are clean and uncracked. Look for eggs that have a "use-by" date stamped on their shells so that you know they are fresh and how long it is safe to store them.
■ Store eggs, pointed-ends down, in the refrigerator, away from strong-smelling foods.
■ Always wash hands thoroughly before and after handling raw eggs.
■ If an egg is contaminated with the salmonella bacteria, the risk of contracting salmonella poisoning is higher if the egg is raw, has a runny yolk or is softly set, so avoid serving these to pregnant women, babies and young children, the sick and elderly. For the salmonella bacteria to be destroyed, the egg must be cooked to 71°C, the temperature at which an egg yolk sets.

DRIED BEANS & PEAS
■ These pulses, especially red kidney beans, may contain harmful toxins, which can cause food poisoning.
■ Always boil dried beans and peas rapidly for a full 10 minutes at the start of the cooking time – this will destroy any toxins.

MEAT
■ Always buy fresh meat from a reputable source and refrigerate it as soon as possible after purchase, first removing any plastic wrappings, drip trays, etc. Put fresh meat on a plate or in a bowl, cover it and place it in the bottom of the refrigerator.
■ Store raw and cooked meats separately and never handle them together. Wash surfaces, utensils and hands before, in between and after dealing with raw and cooked meats.
■ Frozen meat should be defrosted thoroughly before cooking. Throw the thawed liquid away and do not re-freeze raw meat.
■ Only reheat previously cooked meat dishes once. Make sure they are thoroughly reheated until boiling or piping hot (above 75°C).

MUSSELS & CLAMS
■ Buy live mussels and clams from a reputable fishmonger, and cook them on the day of purchase.
■ Before cooking, discard any with broken shells or open shells that do not close when sharply tapped. These are not safe to eat. After cooking, discard any that are not open. These may not be safe either.

POTATOES
■ If potatoes have been exposed to light during storage they may develop green patches, so always store them in the dark as soon as possible after purchase.
■ Small green patches on the skin of potatoes can be cut out with a peeler or knife, but if the greening covers a large area, it is advisable to throw the potato away. Greening can cause stomach upsets.

POULTRY
■ Refrigerate whole birds and pieces as quickly as possible after purchase. Remove any wrappings, and any giblets from the cavity of whole birds, then put the poultry on a plate, cover loosely, and store in the bottom of the refrigerator away from any cooked poultry or meat. Refrigerate any giblets separately in a covered bowl.
■ Poultry is particularly susceptible to contamination by salmonella. Wash work surfaces, utensils and hands thoroughly before and after handling, and do not let the raw bird or any equipment come into contact with cooked poultry or meat.
■ Defrost all birds thoroughly before cooking (for times, see page 160). Do not refreeze.
■ Do not stuff a bird until just before cooking: make sure the stuffing is cold, stuff only the neck end, not the cavity, and keep the stuffing loose.
■ Cook the bird thoroughly to kill any bacteria. At the end of cooking, insert a skewer in the thigh: if properly cooked, the juices should be clear, not pink. Test a large bird with a meat thermometer – the internal temperature should be 90°C.

RICE (COOKED)
■ Always store any leftover cooked rice in a covered container in the refrigerator; never leave it in an uncovered pan or bowl at room temperature. Bacteria, which can cause stomach upsets, can grow in cooked rice if it is not stored at a temperature below 4°C (the temperature of your refrigerator should be between 0°C and 4°C). When reheating cooked rice, make sure it is very hot.

Nutritional Information

The recipes in the Master Recipes and Recipe Repertoire sections all give values for fat, sodium and calories. All figures are approximate and are based on figures from food composition tables with additional data for manufactured products. They are intended as a guide only and not as an absolute amount. All recipes have been analysed with no added salt, unless a specific amount is given in the recipe. The use of salt to taste will result in widely varying sodium levels. Garnishes and ingredients that are described as "to serve" or "optional" are not included in the nutritional analysis.

Conversion Charts

Oven Temperatures

■ Always preheat the oven: if the oven is not preheated before the food goes in, results may not be successful. Recipes in this book have been tested in a preheated oven.

■ Only Celsius temperatures and their Gas Mark equivalents are given in this book; the chart (right) gives the Fahrenheit equivalents. No two ovens are alike, so you may need to adjust temperatures and/or cooking times to suit your oven. For fan ovens, lower the temperatures given in the chart by 10–20°C, according to the manufacturer's handbook.

Celsius	Fahrenheit	Gas	Oven Heat
110°	225°	¼	very cool
120°	250°	½	very cool
140°	275°	1	cool
150°	300°	2	cool
160°	325°	3	moderate
180°	350°	4	moderate
190°	375°	5	moderately hot
200°	400°	6	moderately hot
220°	425°	7	hot
230°	450°	8	very hot

Weights & Measures

■ All of the weights, volumes and measurements in this book are given in metric only. The charts (right) give the imperial equivalents. The two are not interchangeable, so use metric only or imperial only, and never mix them.

■ Tablespoon and teaspoon measures used in this book are expressed as tbsp and tsp, and fractions of these. Recipes have been tested using a set of accurate measuring spoons (see page 26) and spoons are always level unless otherwise stated.

Spoon	Metric
1 tbsp	15ml
1 tsp	5ml
½ tsp	2.5ml
¼ tsp	1.25ml

WEIGHT		VOLUME		MEASUREMENTS	
Metric	Imperial	Metric	Imperial	Metric	Imperial
15g	½oz	125ml	4fl oz	5mm	¼ in
25g	1oz	150ml	¼ pint	1cm	½ in
50g	2oz	175ml	6fl oz	2.5cm	1in
75g	3oz	250ml	8fl oz	5cm	2ins
100g	4oz	275ml	9fl oz	7cm	3ins
175g	6oz	300ml	½ pint	10cm	4ins
200g	7oz	350ml	12fl oz	12cm	5ins
250g	8oz	400ml	14fl oz	15cm	6ins
275g	9oz	450ml	¾ pint	18cm	7ins
300g	10oz	475ml	16fl oz	20cm	8ins
350g	12oz	600ml	1 pint	23cm	9ins
500g	1lb	750ml	1¼ pints	25cm	10ins
750g	1½lb	900ml	1½ pints	28cm	11ins
1kg	2lb	1 litre	1¾ pints	30cm	12ins

INDEX

Page numbers in bold indicate Techniques or Master Recipes; those in italics indicate dishes from the Recipe Repertoire and variations.

An asterisk (*) indicates savoury recipes suitable for vegetarians (replacing chicken stock with vegetable stock where necessary).

ACKNOWLEDGMENTS

FOOD PREPARATION AND RECIPE TESTING
Caroline Liddell

Dorling Kindersley would like to thank Fay Franklin for editorial management, Virginia Walter for design management, Mari Roberts for editorial assistance, Robert Ford and Laura Jackson for design assistance, Susan Bosanko for the index, Jasmine Challis for the nutritional information, and the British Chicken Information Service and the Meat and Livestock Commission for their helpful advice and information.
Additional photography by David Murray and Jules Selmes, Jerry Young, Amanda Heywood, Clive Streeter, Philip Dowell, Stephen Oliver and Steve Gorton.

Special thanks also go to the following companies for their generous gifts: Schwartz Herbs and Spices for the supply of the herbs and spices on pages 14–16; Lakeland Plastics Ltd of Windermere, Cumbria, for the supply of a wide range of kitchen equipment (mail order 015394 88100); ICTC of Norwich for pots, pans and utensils (for information on stockists call 01603 488019); Jim Wilkinson Promotions Ltd for the Good Grips potato masher. Also to the following for their kind loans: Magimix UK Ltd for the blender and food processor; Kenwood Appliances plc for the food mixer (enquiries 01705 476000); Braun (UK) Ltd for the hand-held blender; David Mellor for various items (mail order 0171 730 4259) and Divertimenti for various items (mail order 0171 386 9911).